THE HERE
—AND—
NOW
—HABIT—

*How Mindfulness Can Help
You Break Unhealthy Habits
Once and for All*

Hugh G. Byrne, PhD

New Harbinger Publications, Inc.

Publisher's Note

Excerpt from "Peace Is This Moment Without Judgment" by Dorothy Hunt. Copyright © Dorothy Hunt. Text of "Clearing" by Martha Postlewaite. Copyright © Martha Postlewaite. " Used by permission of the authors.

Excerpt from "Kindness" from WORDS UNDER THE WORDS: SELECTED POEMS by Naomi Shihab Nye. Copyright © 1995 Naomi Shihab Nye / Far Corner Books. Used by permission of the author.

"The Guest House" from THE ESSENTIAL RUMI by Jalal al-Din Rumi, translated by Coleman Barks. Copyright © 1997 by Coleman Barks. Used by permission of Coleman Barks.

Distributed in Canada by Raincoast Books

Copyright © 2016 by Hugh G. Byrne
    New Harbinger Publications, Inc.
    5674 Shattuck Avenue
    Oakland, CA 94609
    www.newharbinger.com

Cover design by Amy Shoup

Acquired by Wendy Millstine

Edited by Will DeRooy

All Rights Reserved

Library of Congress Cataloging-in-Publication Data on file

Printed in the United States of America

18   17   16

10   9   8   7   6   5   4   3   2   1   First printing

To my mother,
Kathleen Byrne,
with
love and gratitude

Contents

Foreword   vii

Introduction   1

Part 1: Laying the Groundwork

1   Understanding Habits   9

2   The Basics of Mindfulness   27

Part 2: Putting Wisdom into Practice

3   The Power of Intention: What Matters Most?   53

4   Welcoming Your "Guests"   65

5   Cultivating Attitudes of Mindfulness   77

6   Harnessing the Power of Attention   95

7   Untangling Yourself from Habitual
Thoughts and Beliefs   117

8   Riding the Waves of Emotions, Urges,
and Cravings   133

9   Taking In the Good: Cultivating Emotions
That Support Well-Being and Happiness   145

10   Breaking Harmful Habits in Your
Relationships and the Wider World   163

Conclusion: Making Mindfulness Your
Default Habit   175

Acknowledgments   181

References   183

Foreword

I was in college, in the midst of final exams, when I first heard the phrase "How you live today is how you live your life." My mind immediately fixated on my exhaustion after pulling an all-nighter to study, the fact that I hadn't taken a run for a week, and judgmental thoughts surrounding a recent ice cream binge. The notion that these habits reflected my life was disturbing. Yet, over time, what at first seemed jarring and oppressive became empowering. The shift came in realizing that today, right in this very moment, we can deepen our attention and cultivate habits that support healing and freedom.

Our habits—how we think, speak, feel, and act—directly impact our well-being. More broadly, they reinforce patterns that shape our entire experience of living. Our habits determine whether we are available to listen when our child is trying to communicate and how well we can take care of our own bodies and minds as we age. Our habits determine whether we bring our full intelligence to what we do and whether we are able to enjoy the beauty and mystery of the moment. If we want to live a life in which we are true to ourselves, remembering what matters most to us and expressing our natural creativity and love, we need to honestly examine our current habits.

Habits are like the streams that create riverbeds: with a steady flow of water, channels become deep grooves. And yet, if the flow is redirected, rivers can be rerouted. Neuroplasticity makes this possible: the pathways in our brain—including the riverbeds of habits that affect our well-being—can be altered depending on how we direct our attention. Where attention goes, energy flows. A mindful awareness is essential in guiding the flow in ways that will help us realize our full potential.

Buddhist teachings, contemporary psychology, and recent findings in neuroscience all converge on a simple principle: By bringing mindful attention to our habits of thought, feeling, speech, and action, we can transform even the most painful and limiting patterns. In order to make changes, we need to witness our habits with an engaged, nonjudging presence and a tender, caring heart.

From an evolutionary perspective, the capacity for mindfulness is a recent development; it emerged—along with empathy, compassion, and executive thinking skills—with the growth of our brain's frontal cortex. Without mindfulness, our habits would be entirely driven by the primitive energies of attraction (desire) and aversion (fear). Mindfulness enables us to evolve our consciousness and influence our subsequent life experience by bringing awareness to the habits that keep us from achieving our potential. With mindfulness, we can identify the impulses behind our automatic and reactive behaviors and see the way they impact our lives and the people around us. With mindfulness, we can cultivate habits that will help us fulfill our hearts' deepest intentions.

There are a number of fine books on strategies for changing your habits, and there is a growing literature on meditation. The book you have in your hands addresses the dynamic and essential intersection of these two areas: applying mindfulness to habits. Author Hugh Byrne, a good friend and deeply respected colleague who has helped thousands of students make positive, lasting changes, is an ideal guide for investigating this terrain. In a clear and accessible style, drawing on three decades of meditation practice and more than fifteen years of teaching mindfulness, Hugh will help you understand the most recent scientific research related to habits and introduce you to state-of-the-art strategies for supporting habit change. You'll learn skills to address addictive behaviors, barriers to intimacy, harsh self-judgment, procrastination, and other forms of self-sabotage.

Most importantly, you'll discover that even the most challenging habits will transform as you bring a caring presence to your inner life. Hugh will show you how, by practicing mindfulness, you can develop a wise, healing relationship with the unmet needs that drive unhelpful habits. This will prepare the ground for you to cultivate new habits that endow every aspect of your life with more presence, joy, and ease.

Remember the phrase that caught my attention in college? I now reflect on a slightly different version: "How you live *this moment* is how you live your life." If you embrace the practices in this book, this moment becomes a place of profound possibility. In this moment, you can choose to offer a compassionate attention to unproductive, limiting habits; in this moment, you can further manifest your full capacity for love and wisdom. *The Here-and-Now Habit* offers an ideal map for this journey. May it help you find meaning and freedom in your life.

—Tara Brach, PhD
Author, *Radical Acceptance* and *True Refuge*

Introduction

It has been said that we teach best what we most need to learn. This has been my experience as I have studied how habits form and why they can be so hard to change—and as I have explored the role of mindfulness in changing my own unhealthy habits.

I have practiced mindfulness for more than twenty-five years, and the benefits have been profound. Mindfulness has helped bring more peace, acceptance, and ease into my life, and it has reduced my stress and suffering. But until recently, I was still unaware of certain habits of mine (this tends to be the nature of habits—they operate "under the radar") that were causing suffering. It was only as I dug into the research on habits and their power—and turned the spotlight of my attention inward—that I came to see certain patterns of thought and behavior that led to stress and disconnection. I noticed how, for example, in situations where I needed to wait—in stores, on the phone, in traffic—I frequently experienced unpleasant sensations of tension, tightness, and feeling confined, accompanied by the thought *I need to change this*, and I responded by acting impatiently.

I also became aware of a habit of putting off tasks and responsibilities that felt difficult or challenging and only engaging with them when they became truly urgent. Though not a chronic procrastinator, I experienced low-level tension and worry about things I needed to take care of.

Another personal habit I observed was a tendency toward distraction. I saw how, if I wasn't consciously being present, my attention easily went to whatever was most visible, audible, shiny, or exciting. (My partner, Rebecca, often found this challenging—for example, when my attention would go to a new message on my iPad while we were cooking together.)

Perhaps my most challenging personal habit was that, when the demands and pressures of life became intense, I would get caught up in anxious, worried thinking: *How am I going to get all this done?* This led, at times, to difficult periods in which I kept thinking there was too much to do and not enough time.

Bringing mindfulness to these habits—and reflecting on how I had been able to let go of earlier unhealthy habits, such as smoking and overeating—showed me the power of awareness in transforming unhelpful and unwanted habits.

I don't mean to say that it's a done deal and all my unhealthy habits are in the past. But I have learned—from my own experience and from working with many of my mindfulness students—that mindfulness is the best path to healthier habits and a life of greater freedom and ease.

Almost all of us have developed or will develop habits that are unhealthy or don't truly serve our interests or meet our needs. We all grapple with patterns of thinking and behavior that can be hard to change. Mindful awareness can help you abandon unhealthy patterns and create new, healthier ones. Whether you overeat, smoke, think negatively, work too much, get lost in distractions like social media and TV, or are a heavy user of alcohol or other substances, the mindfulness practices in this book can help you free yourself from these patterns and heal your mind and heart.

Mindfulness is not a quick fix. Anyone who suggests that changing habits is quick or easy is selling snake oil. Just as habits—both healthy and unhealthy ones—take time to form, they take time and effort to change.

Mindfulness is a practice—a training of the mind—that you cultivate over time, with effort and determination. But, as you'll see, mindfulness—*conscious awareness* of your present-moment experience—is a natural antidote to unhealthy habits, which are *unconscious and automatic*. Mindfulness will open the way for you, so that you can make choices that are more healthy and helpful. Then, once the choices you make about how to act and live align with your true interests and well-being, you can live more freely.

Right now, perhaps you think that your unhealthy or unhelpful habits reflect some essential truth about who you are. When considering your unwanted habits, you may think *Something is wrong with me, I'm flawed*, or even *I'm a bad person*. Perhaps you have tried to change your habits and concluded that you're weak or ineffective or a failure. However, unwanted habits are the result of natural processes rather than character flaws. They arise from your attempts to meet your needs—for example, your need for comfort or your need for safety or security.

If a behavior you embark on in an attempt to meet a need has powerful short-term benefits—even if it has long-term drawbacks—you're likely to repeat that behavior. That's

3

because your mind is mostly concerned with how you feel *right now*, and in that sense, the immediate comfort of lighting a cigarette or relaxing on the couch in front of the TV feels more compelling than the adverse health effects of smoking or not getting enough exercise. When repeated regularly under consistent conditions, the behavior becomes automatic and unconscious—and challenging to change.

Think of having unhealthy habits as having lost your way: you're on a path that doesn't lead to where you want to go. Your task is to find your way home—to bring your thoughts and actions into alignment with your intentions and your deepest needs. Mindfulness offers a reliable and trustworthy path home; the mindful skills of attention, kindness, and acceptance can help you transform unhealthy habits into a way of being that embodies freedom and inner peace.

This book is divided into two parts. In part 1 (chapters 1 and 2), we'll examine how habits form and why they can be difficult to change. You'll see how mindfulness, by bringing what has become unconscious and automatic into the light of your awareness, can provide a unique road map to habit change. I'll outline four main types of habit: habits of *wanting*—craving or seeking food, drink, sex, or any other object of desire; habits of *distraction*—checking out from your experience and into something more attractive or exciting, such as social media or TV; habits of *resisting*—attempting to distance yourself from things you find unpleasant or difficult; and habits of *doing*—feeling stressed, always on your way to somewhere else, disconnected from the present.

Understanding the brain and how habits form is only the first step. In order to change your ingrained patterns of behavior, you'll need to purposely train your mind to abandon unhelpful patterns of thought and behavior while you learn to cultivate more life-affirming habits. To that end, chapters 3 through 9 present mindfulness practices and guided meditations to help you let go of unhealthy habits, cultivate more beneficial habits, increase your happiness, and live with more ease. (To download audio tracks for these practices, visit the New Harbinger Publications website at http://www.newhar binger.com/32370, or see the back of this book.) Practitioners have "road-tested" these practices and meditations for more than two thousand years and discovered their power to support happiness and well-being. Recent findings from neuroscience confirm what mindfulness practitioners have long known: that mindfulness brings about positive changes in the brain and supports improvements in mental and emotional health.

In Chapter 10 we'll examine how unhealthy habits in communication can lead to interpersonal problems, and we'll look at some practices for applying mindfulness to your communications. Then we'll consider ways of transforming harmful collective habits and beliefs that we may absorb unconsciously as members of certain groups in society. We'll conclude with some tips for establishing a regular practice of meditation and bringing mindfulness into your daily life.

A note on language: I don't use the term "bad habits" in this book, because labeling a pattern of thought or action as "bad" tends to solidify it and imply that it's something you need to rid yourself of or push away.

It's more helpful to label habits based on their consequences. If a habit causes harm, as with smoking or addiction to alcohol or drugs, a better term than "bad" is "harmful." If a habit has negative health consequences—as stress and anxiety frequently do, a better term than "bad" is "unhealthy." If a habitual way of thinking or acting isn't necessarily harmful or unhealthy, but you feel it doesn't serve your goals or intentions, a better term than "bad" is "unhelpful" or "unwanted."

Mindfulness invites you to kindly and curiously bring your attention to whatever you're experiencing—thoughts, emotions, urges, impulses, sensations—and to see that these phenomena are not inherently "good" or "bad," but rather impersonal and transient. The key to finding freedom in the midst of challenging and difficult experiences is to meet them with acceptance and compassion. Describing a habit you'd like to change as "unhealthy," "harmful," "unhelpful," or "unwanted" will support a kind and nonjudging relationship to your experience.

I invite you to explore these skills and practices and see for yourself.

PART 1

LAYING THE GROUNDWORK

CHAPTER 1

Understanding Habits

We become what we repeatedly do.

—Sean Covey, *The 7 Habits of Highly Effective Teens*

You probably consider yourself as a rational being whose life is guided by your choices, plans, and intentions. When you choose to eat something sweet or check your e-mail or take a particular route to work, you're doing so because you have made a conscious choice—or so you think.

You might be surprised to know that almost half the time, you do what you do because you have done it before under similar circumstances. Researchers have found that between a third and half of all behaviors tend to be repeated in the same physical location every day (Wood, Quinn, and Kashy 2002, 1286). In other words, they're habits.

Understanding how habits form, why they can be hard to change, and potential ways to transform them is an important step to finding greater freedom and peace. The better you understand habits and the more you shine the light of your own awareness on them, the more you'll be empowered to bring your actions into alignment with your deepest values. This ability can be a source of freedom and power.

What Are Habits?

Habits are behaviors that have developed through repetition over time. They're things you have done so often that you now do them automatically. The philosopher William James wrote 125 years ago:

> Any sequence of mental action which has been frequently repeated tends to perpetuate itself; so that we find ourselves automatically prompted to think, feel, or do what we have been before accustomed to think, feel, or do, under like circumstances, without any consciously formed purpose, or anticipation of results. (James 1890, 112)

Modern science confirms James's assessment of habits: Repetition of an action in a consistent context leads, over time, to the behavior being activated by contextual cues (time, place, feelings, and so forth), rather than by conscious intention. What that means is that the behavior becomes more like a reflex—one that's triggered by where you are, what time it is, whom you're with, how you're feeling, or what you're thinking. In other words, you carry out the action automatically whenever the circumstances seem to fit. At this point, the behavior is no longer linked directly to your intentions or your original goal. You're unaware or only dimly aware of the reason for the behavior, and you may not even be aware of what you're doing. It's as if you're on autopilot.

But habits aren't an aberration, some glitch in our evolutionary wiring. Charles Duhigg, bestselling author of *The*

Power of Habit: Why We Do What We Do in Life and Business, explains habits as the brain's way of conserving energy, allowing our minds to ramp down more often, and points to the evolutionary benefits:

> An efficient brain requires less room, which makes for a smaller head, which makes childbirth easier and therefore causes fewer infant and mother deaths. An efficient brain also allows us to stop thinking constantly about basic behaviors, such as walking and choosing what to eat, so we can devote mental energy to inventing spears, irrigation systems, and, eventually, airplanes and video games. (Duhigg 2012, 18)

Human beings are creatures of habit, and that's not a bad thing, because habits aren't inherently good or bad. Habits typically begin as behaviors undertaken to achieve a goal. For example, you drive to the train station to take a train to get to work; you brush and floss your teeth to prevent cavities and support good health; or you eat a bowl of ice cream for comfort when you feel lonely or bored.

Habit formation is intended to help us be efficient. Think how much more complex and stressful our lives would be if all our everyday activities were the subject of deliberation and decision-making. Driving a car, for example, would be a much more complex and challenging activity if we had to relearn the rules of the road every time we got behind the wheel.

Still, sometimes our habits run counter to our long-term goals, needs, and values. It's easy to develop habits that bring you comfort but don't serve you or don't reflect your deepest needs. Habits may distance you from your own life, or they may prevent you from achieving a deeper connection with your loved ones and the world. They may at times be harmful, unhealthy, and even deadly.

The Price We Pay for Unhealthy Habits

Following are some common unhealthy habits:

- Eating, drinking alcohol, using drugs, using tobacco, having sex, shopping, overworking, or gambling to comfort yourself or avoid feeling something unpleasant (for example, anxiety, loneliness, or uncertainty)

- Compulsively or continually checking your messages, going online, or watching TV, which saps your time and energy and causes you to be absent from your life, your family, and the present moment

- Acting out angrily in thought, word, or action in ways that cause pain to yourself or others (for example, getting frustrated with staff in stores or on the phone; driving impatiently; sending angry e-mails; feeling annoyed or angry with family members, friends, or colleagues; or judging yourself or others negatively)

- Feeling as if you're forever on the go, on your way somewhere, or crossing things off a to-do list

- Worrying about the future and imagining negative or scary scenarios

- Spending large amounts of time ruminating on the past—how you acted, what you might have done differently, or what people have done to you

- Procrastinating (finding ways to put off particular tasks or projects you need to complete)

These habits may be causing you suffering and harming others as well. At the very least, they don't serve your needs, your long-term goals, or your deepest intentions. Think of the ways in which a constant need to be online can separate you from your loved ones, or how mindless snacking can leave you feeling judgmental and separated from yourself. Consumerism can keep you locked in patterns that conflict with your deepest sense of what's good for you. Even habits of distraction, like biting your nails or humming or picking your fingers when you're feeling nervous or anxious, prevent you from being fully present for your life—experiencing the passing joys and sorrows in various moments.

Roy's Story

One of my students, Roy, has quit cigarettes, alcohol, and drugs. But a long-time source of suffering for Roy—one that has been compared to heroin (Avena, Rada, and Hoebel 2008)—remains: a craving for sweets, which visits him most strongly in the hour or two before bedtime. Most evenings Roy eats a large bowl of ice cream or a plate of cookies even though he's a diabetic, and afterward he feels bad both physically and emotionally.

Roy's craving is familiar to many. Michael Moss, in his powerful book *Salt, Sugar, Fat: How the Food Giants Hooked Us*, points out: "There are special receptors for sweetness in every one of the mouth's ten thousand taste buds, and they are all hooked up, one way or another, to the parts of the brain known as the pleasure zones, where we get rewarded for stoking our bodies with energy" (Moss 2014, 3–4). (We'll come back to Roy's efforts to work with his sugar habit in later chapters.)

In addition to the drawbacks mentioned above, some unhealthy habits have extraordinarily high social costs, as shown in statistics for addictions rooted in unhealthy habitual behaviors:

- Tobacco use is the leading cause of preventable death in the United States. Worldwide, tobacco use accounts for five million preventable deaths a year—some 10 percent of deaths overall (Brewer et al. 2011).

- Alcohol consumption, illicit drugs, and obesity account for an additional 21 percent of preventable deaths in the United States (Adams et al. 2014; Bowen and Marlatt 2009).

- Substance abuse and addiction cost more than $600 billion annually (including productivity and health- and crime-related costs)—illegal drugs, $193 billion; alcohol, $235 billion; and tobacco use, $193 billion (NIH 2012). "As staggering as these numbers are, they do not fully describe the breadth of destructive public health and safety implications of drug abuse and addiction, such as family disintegration, loss of employment, failure in school, domestic violence, and child abuse" (NIH 2012, n.p.).

- The incidence of obesity (key causes of which lie in unhealthy eating habits and insufficient physical activity) in the United States has increased from 13 percent to 34 percent in the past fifty years, and obesity accounts for $190 billion in medical costs alone (Begley 2012).

- More than 40 percent of people between 19 and 39 years old say they text while they drive, and 10 percent say they do so regularly. Driving while distracted by smartphones and other devices caused 3,331 deaths and 387,000 injuries in 2011 (Neyfakh 2013; Halsey 2013).

In our individual lives, unhealthy and unwanted habits can cause intense physical, mental, emotional, and spiritual suffering. When we act in ways that are out of alignment with our values, intentions, and deepest needs, we suffer. And unsuccessful attempts to change behavior—often caused by lack of awareness of the power of habits and the most effective ways of changing them—can engender a sense of failure, guilt, disappointment, or resignation, helping perpetuate unhealthy behaviors.

It's Hard to Change Established Habits

Almost all of us, if we look at our lives honestly, have habits and patterns that we would like to change. Have you ever found yourself repeatedly doing something that you know doesn't reflect the best of who you are? Have you ever thought, *Why do I keep doing this?* Perhaps you have made plans or resolutions to kick this habit, but found yourself falling back or relapsing—and then felt disappointed with yourself.

Here are some common habits that are hard to change:

- Eating too much or too often—not from hunger, but to numb an emotion or to feel a sense of comfort

- Spending long hours on social media or checking your e-mail, knowing this isn't the best use of your time and energy

- Smoking cigarettes, despite the serious health costs

- Working long hours as a way of avoiding other areas of your life

- Getting caught up in negative or judgmental thoughts about yourself or others

If you develop unhealthy or harmful habits, it doesn't mean you're flawed or that you have failed somehow. You have simply lost connection with your true interests and intentions, possibly mistaking short-term relief from unpleasant or uncomfortable feelings for real happiness and well-being.

Intuitively, you might think that once you recognize that a behavior was unhealthy or unwanted, and you decide to change it, you should be able to modify your behavior so that your actions and habits correspond with your intentions and goals. But it's not so simple, because there are two separate behavioral systems in your brain.

According to Nobel Prize–winning psychologist Daniel Kahneman, there are two modes of "cognitive function": an intuitive mode (which he calls System 1), in which judgments and decisions are made automatically and rapidly, and a controlled mode (which he calls System 2), which is deliberate and slower.

> The operations of System 1 are…often emotionally charged; they are also governed by habit and are therefore difficult to control or modify. The operations of System 2 are…more likely to be consciously monitored and deliberately controlled; they are also relatively flexible. (Kahneman 2003, 698)

Walter Mischel, a psychologist renowned for his studies of children's abilities to defer gratification (for example, by not eating a marshmallow right away, in order to get an extra marshmallow), calls these two brain systems the *hot emotional system* and the *cool cognitive system* (Mischel 2014).

What's more, these systems don't always coordinate well. The "hot" brain system responds more quickly, and its messages are more compelling than those of the "cool" brain system. Thus when your intentions and plans (the workings of the "cool" brain system) conflict with your firmly established habits (the workings of the "hot" brain system), your habits tend to win out.

Studies involving blood donation, use of seat belts, modes of travel, and fast-food consumption show that as habit strength increases, intentions play less of a role in predicting behavior (Nilsen et al. 2012). As one study noted, "Essentially, habits yield tunnel vision, thus reducing the effectiveness of interventions aimed at changing behaviour through conscious cognitive deliberation" (Nilsen et al. 2012, 2).

Does the persistence of habits in the face of intentions to change them mean that we're doomed to keep repeating them? Is habit destiny? Clearly not. Most of us have changed unwanted behaviors, and you probably know people who have transformed deeply painful and entrenched habits. You *can* consciously develop habits that are aligned with your intentions and goals. If you wish to develop a healthy habit, you need to repeat the desired behavior in a consistent context until the behavior becomes automatic. Recent studies suggest that it takes about sixty-six days to develop a new habit (Gardner 2012). If you want to abandon an unhealthy or unwanted habit, you have to find ways to disrupt and discontinue the automatic behavior.

The Here-and-Now Habit

Studies have shown that certain conditions and processes aid changing unwanted habits and developing more productive and beneficial ones:

- Changes in the environment can support shifting from habit mode into more intentional or planned behaviors. For example, when the context changes (taking a vacation, moving to a new residence, or changing colleges), the "cues" that trigger habitual behaviors may be absent or less available, resulting in greater potential for new behaviors to be guided by intentions (Nilsen et al. 2012).

- Taking steps to circumvent the "cues" that trigger habitual behaviors can support habit change. For example, an alcoholic in recovery might choose to avoid oft-frequented drinking places or old drinking buddies, or a person who's trying to eat healthily might walk or drive home by a different route to avoid a donut shop or fast-food restaurant (Quinn et al. 2010).

- To act in keeping with your intentions in the face of strong habits, your intentions need to be strong and clear. When intentions come into conflict with strong habits, behaviors are likely to be directed by intentions only if held "with sufficient strength and implemented with sufficient skill to override well-practiced behavior," as one influential study of habits and intentions proposed (Ouellette and Wood 1998, 7).

- One of the most effective ways to change harmful habits and ensure that your actions are in keeping with your values and goals is to establish "implementation intentions"—plans of action that specify the exact behaviors you'll take in response to specific cues. For example, "as soon as the six o'clock news is over I will switch off the TV, put on my running shoes and go out for a thirty-minute run" (Gollwitzer and Schaal 1998).

- Anticipating difficulties and envisioning ways of responding to them increase the possibility of successful habit change. For example, a person attempting to lose weight might imagine how he or she would respond in a social situation where high-calorie food was offered (Quinn et al. 2010).

- Change is less likely if the person hasn't already committed to change. Studies have shown that a person who at the start of a smoking cessation program is actively preparing to quit smoking or already taking steps to quit is almost twice as likely to succeed in quitting as someone who at the start of a smoking cessation program is only contemplating quitting (Prochaska, DiClemente, and Norcross 1992).

- "Vigilantly monitoring" habitual behaviors (such as actively watching yourself for the behavior and thinking *Don't do it*) heightens cognitive control and is an effective way of inhibiting strong habits (Quinn et al. 2010).

Most of the common means of making changes, including methods developed by psychologists and health professionals, aim to alter habits by establishing new plans and intentions—for example, setting yourself the goal, "I'm going to eat healthy food instead of junk food." But although intentions are crucial to habit change, in order to be effective they need to be very clear and specific, and they need to be supported by strong practices of self-awareness. This involves making what's largely invisible visible, by intentionally and mindfully bringing into conscious awareness habitual patterns of thought and behavior.

The Power of Mindfulness to Change Unwanted Habits

Through *mindfulness*—an approach for bringing a kind and nonjudging awareness to your moment-to-moment experience, rooted in centuries of Buddhist teachings and practice—you can change even long-established and seemingly entrenched habits.

This book provides mindfulness skills and practices for letting go of old habits and creating new, healthier habits and healthier ways of living. Mindfulness gives you the power to transform your behaviors because it shines a light on whatever is happening *in the moment*—including thoughts you normally aren't aware of and things you normally don't notice yourself doing.

Mindfulness is both a training and a practice. Since habits develop through repetition over time, it's rarely enough to clearly see your unhealthy patterns just a few times. You need to create new patterns—and new neural pathways in your brain—that can help you learn to identify unwanted or harmful habits. You need to learn to accept and let yourself experience challenging sensations, emotions, and mind states. You also need to cultivate kindness and compassion toward yourself, because they're the key to freedom and to healing from the stresses of being caught up in painful habits. In chapter 2 we'll look at ways in which mindfulness can be an antidote to habitual behavior and provide a powerful path to changing unhealthy habits.

Before we go any further, however, it's important that you identify a habit or habits that you would like to change. There may be an obvious area for you to work on, perhaps a behavior you have already tried to change. If not, or to help you identify behaviors that may be affecting your life in negative or painful ways, try the following practice.

Practice 1: Identifying Habits That Don't Serve Your Well-Being

This activity is meant to help you reflect on activities or areas of your life in which you're not fully present.

Over the coming week, with kindness and without judging yourself, take some time each day to write down your responses to the following questions, perhaps in a notebook. (It can be helpful to keep a notebook for responding to the practices in this book and for recording any insights that come to you as you read about and practice mindfulness.)

- At what times are you on autopilot?

- At what times do your actions or thoughts have negative consequences for your health, relationships, or overall well-being?

- Is there something you do that you feel is unhealthy or compulsive or that separates or isolates you from others? Something that's not in alignment with how you want to live your life?

- If there's a habit that seems unhealthy or that you'd like to change, how do you feel (in your body and your mind)

21

when you carry out this habit? What are you aware of before, during, and after carrying out the habit? Is there tension, pleasure, numbness, judgment? Simply notice whatever is present, and write it down.

• In what ways does this habit cause you stress, pain, difficulty, or suffering? Does it separate you from your family, from your friends, or from yourself? Does it feel out of alignment with how you want to live? Does it leave you feeling guilty, self-critical, or regretful? Do you feel physically uncomfortable afterward—as with a smoker's cough, a hangover, or the feeling of having eaten too much?

• What need do you think this behavior or way of thinking fills for you? If it doesn't serve a need now, what need did it meet for you at some point? Is there another way, or ways, you could achieve the original goal or objective of this behavior? Visualize how you might feel if you abandoned this unhealthy habit. As you imagine yourself no longer practicing this unhealthy habit, notice how you feel both physically and emotionally. Notice the thoughts that arise.

• Is there a healthy or helpful habit that could replace your current habit? It might be an alternative behavior, such as eating fruit or nuts instead of eating candy, or simply not doing what you have been doing and learning to stay with whatever feelings are present.

• At this time, how strong is your commitment to changing this habit or developing a new habit? How important is it to you personally? If the answer is less than "very," it's likely that your old ways will prevail. Take some time to reflect on the potential benefits of making a change. Think about potential obstacles to breaking this habit, and envision effective ways of responding if these obstacles or other challenges arise. Would talking about your commitment with and seeking support from a family member or friend help you make this change?

Throughout the upcoming chapters, our discussion of mindfulness will often center on one or more of six common habits that are challenging to change:

- Smoking

- Worry and anxiety

- Procrastination

- Aggressive and unmindful driving

- Unhealthy and unmindful eating

- Overuse of electronics

I'll illustrate how specific mindfulness skills can help bring about change in these and many other habitual ways of thinking and acting.

I want to be clear that in the case of these last two habits, we'll be focusing on the "unconsciousness" and the negative consequences involved as what makes these habits unwanted or unhealthy. Regarding eating, if there are no health issues involved, having a donut or a slice of cheesecake can be harmless or even contribute to your emotional well-being. Regarding use of electronics, computers provide great benefits—thanks to the Internet, thousands of meditations (including the ones created for this book) and talks on mindfulness and related themes are available to anyone at the click of a button. And in recent months I have found myself walking about twice as much as I had previously, thanks to an app on my phone that has made me more conscious of how much exercise I'm getting.

In fact, how much any habit is detrimental has to do with the consciousness or unconsciousness with which you do it. When it comes to drinking a glass of wine, for example, you can drink mindfully, paying attention to the experience, or you can drink without paying attention, in a way that makes it easy to become dependent on the habit (with negative consequences). The more activities you do consciously, the more opportunities you'll have to make choices that truly benefit you.

Understanding Habits—Summing Up

Almost half of our actions are habitual in nature: performed in an automatic way and activated by contextual cues rather than conscious intention. Habits help us simplify and organize our lives—life would be infinitely more complex if we had to think about and make decisions about the many aspects of all our daily activities. By making our brains more efficient, habits have helped humans become who we are today. Habits have helped us travel to the moon and paint the Sistine Chapel.

But almost all of us have habits that we'd like to change because they don't serve us or because they don't reflect our deepest values, goals, or intentions. Unhealthy habits and addictions like tobacco, drug and alcohol abuse, and distracted driving carry huge social costs, both in terms of lives lost and in terms of economic resources that could be better spent. Getting caught up in even seemingly harmless automatic behaviors can actually have a very high cost: we can miss out on our children, our family, and our lives.

Changing well-established habits is difficult. When an intention to change a behavior confronts a strong habit, the habit often wins, because the messages coming from the "cool" cognitive brain system are slower and less urgent than those coming from the "hot" emotional brain system.

Understanding how habits form and operate, and why they can be so resistant to change, is key to changing them. Also essential is bringing awareness to your direct experience through mindfulness. Mindfulness gets to the heart of habitual behaviors and gives you a means of releasing yourself from their grip. Mindfulness can help you become aware of patterns of behavior that have become automatic and unconscious. It can help you bring unconscious thoughts and behaviors into consciousness and render the invisible visible.

CHAPTER 2

The Basics of Mindfulness

The essence of mindfulness is to bring the light of attention to all that has been invisible and habitual.

—Christina Feldman,
Compassion: Listening to the Cries of the World

Imagine two very similar but very different scenarios:

Scenario 1: You're walking through the woods on a crisp early autumn day. You see the interplay of light and shade as the sun shines through the leaves swaying in the breeze, and you feel the cool air on your face. You feel the weight of your body on your feet as you walk along the path, and you feel the beating of your heart as the path gets steeper. You hear the chirping of birds, the buzzing of insects, and the distant rumble of a truck. Thoughts of daily life come and go, but they don't interfere with your enjoyment of the simple pleasure of your walk. You feel alive and present, open to your experience and to life.

Scenario 2: You're walking through the woods on a crisp early autumn day. Your mind is caught up in worries about all the work you have to do and fears that something important will fall through the cracks. Your mind is pulled back to the memory of a difficult encounter with your boss earlier in the week and what that might mean for your future. This thought is followed by concerns about the poor grades your teenage son received on his latest report card and worries about the friends he has been hanging out with. You check your phone to see whether any important messages have landed in your inbox since you began your walk. Consumed by your anxious thoughts, you're barely aware of your surroundings. Like a seesaw, your mind alternates between ruminating on the past and worrying about the future. If you stopped to pay attention to what was going on in your body, you might notice that your muscles were tense, reflecting your mental state.

Each moment of our waking lives, we have the opportunity to be present—aware of what's unfolding in our bodies, our hearts, our minds, and our environment—or to be somewhere else. Sages have taught for centuries that being present here and now allows us to feel greater peace, contentment, and joy.

It's easy, though, to develop patterns of thought and behavior that take you away from your present experience— into rumination, worry, and fear, which, in turn, lead to stress and suffering. If you don't practice awareness, it's easy to eat too much, drink too much, or slip into other unhealthy behaviors that offer momentary relief but separate you from your deepest intentions. Mindfulness practices and skills will help you change unhealthy habits and balance your life.

What Mindfulness Involves

Although mindfulness was developed within the Buddhist tradition over the past 2,500 years, it's a universal quality of present-moment awareness that can be experienced and cultivated independent of any particular religion or philosophy.

Have you ever for a moment felt fully alive, engaged, and embodied, connected to yourself, to what you were doing, and to life? Have you been at a concert or a play where you were fully immersed in the action or the music? Or simply walked through your neighborhood or in nature and felt fully present? Mindfulness is being here and knowing you're here, being present here and now, which is a direct path to well-being, happiness, and freedom.

Different forms of mindful awareness exist in many religions:

- Going on pilgrimage, in many traditions

- Walking a labyrinth and centering prayer, in Christian practice

- Kneeling to pray five times a day, in Islam

- Shabbat or the Sabbath as a time of pausing and inner reflection, in Judaism

All of these are ways of "remembering" to come home to yourself and your life. In fact, the Pali word for "mindfulness," *sati*, also means "remembering." (Pali is the language in which the Buddha's teachings were first written—some five hundred years after his death.)

Both in Buddhism and in more secular approaches to mindfulness, you learn to bring awareness consciously and intentionally to your present-moment experience *as it is*, without judgment and with acceptance of whatever arises. It's a more *intentional* and *attentional* focus than you typically bring to your everyday life, in which you may spend much of your time lost in thoughts about the future or the past, daydreaming, or on "autopilot."

Jon Kabat-Zinn, a scientist and meditation teacher who has played a major role in making mindfulness widely accessible in the West, defined mindfulness as "the awareness that emerges through paying attention on purpose, in the present moment, and non-judgmentally to the unfolding of experience moment to moment" (Kabat-Zinn 2003, 145).

Mindfulness is a *quality* of attention or awareness. When you pay attention intentionally and without judgment to your experience, you're being mindful. Mindfulness is also the conscious *practice* of cultivating this quality of attention.

Internationally recognized expert in mindfulness Shauna Shapiro and colleagues (Shapiro et al. 2006) have pointed to three key elements that compose mindfulness: *intention*—why you practice, your motivations and aspirations; *attention*—observing and recognizing what you're experiencing; and *attitude*—the qualities of heart and mind that you bring to attention. These three essential qualities are tools available to anyone who wishes to change unhealthy or unwanted habits.

You can apply mindfulness to any area or activity of your life: you can drive mindfully, walk mindfully, eat mindfully, shower mindfully, be a mindful parent, or be a mindful leader. Through this quality of presence—showing up for your life—you can improve any aspect of your life, including the painful and difficult times.

Mindfulness *meditation* differs from "everyday" mindfulness only in the sense that you formally set aside a time and place to make the practice of mindfulness the focus of your activity. You can practice mindfulness meditation while sitting, standing, walking, or lying down, and while engaged in any kind of formal meditation practice, such as an eating meditation. The importance of formal practice is that it gives you the time and the opportunity to observe and train your mind in a setting of your choosing, where you'll be relatively free of distractions.

The Origins of Mindfulness in Buddhist Teachings

Some 2,500 years ago, Siddhartha Gautama, a man born into nobility in northern India, left his home and family on a quest to discover whether freedom from grief and suffering was possible. He studied with leading teachers of his time and engaged in intense ascetic practices. Then, leaving behind the path of austerity, he meditated through a full-moon night and discovered a "middle way," a path to a complete end to suffering. This was his awakening or enlightenment.

After his awakening and until his death forty-five years later, the Buddha (which translates as "one who has awakened") shared his teachings with people from all walks of life. His teachings have been passed on throughout Asia for a hundred generations by a monastic community, supported by lay followers. Over the past century, and particularly in the last two generations, these teachings have come to the West and are having a profound impact on our society, where a growing body of research points to the beneficial effects of mindfulness.

The Buddha's Teaching on Suffering and the End of Suffering

At the core of all the Buddha's teachings are four basic propositions—the Four Noble Truths. As the Buddha himself recommended, these are to be explored and tested, rather than taken as a set of "beliefs" that must be strictly adhered to.

Suffering—a sense of dissatisfaction or persistent unease—is pervasive in human life. The Buddha taught that birth, death, sickness, aging, and loss are all forms of suffering. This is the First Noble Truth—*the existence of suffering.*

The typical sense of dissatisfaction characteristic of human suffering arises from wanting things to be different. We want more of what we like and less of what we don't like. We experience this as craving, and it leads to suffering. This is the Second Noble Truth—*craving as the cause of suffering.*

When you're willing to be open to your experience just as it is, you'll see that pleasant experiences can't be held onto and that unpleasant experiences also pass. Everything is constantly changing. *You're* constantly changing—you have no stable, permanent "self." Rather, the illusion of a permanent self is created by your mind's clinging to certain ideas about yourself. When you see clearly that trying to cling to anything leads to suffering, you can begin to let go. Letting go completely, accepting things as they really are, is the end of suffering, the goal of the Buddhist path. This is the Third Noble Truth—*the end of suffering: freedom,* or *nirvana.*

The Fourth Noble Truth is the *path to the end of suffering* laid out by the Buddha, called the Noble Eightfold Path. It involves wise (or skillful, or appropriate) cultivation of eight elements: *understanding, intention, speech, action, livelihood, effort, mindfulness,* and *concentration.*

The Role of Mindfulness

Mindfulness plays a central role in Buddhism. In a major teaching on the foundations of mindfulness, the *Satipatthana Sutta,* the Buddha taught that mindfulness is a direct path to freedom from suffering (Anālayo 2003). By bringing mindfulness to four fields of experience—(1) your body; (2) the "feeling tone" (pleasant, unpleasant, or neutral) of your experience; (3) your emotions and mind states; and (4) your subjective reality as experienced through the lens of key Buddhist teachings—you can gain liberating insights. You can come to see the true nature of all experience as changing, impersonal, and unreliable. This insight will lead to the end of clinging and to freedom from suffering. Rather than being in conflict with your situation or experience (that is, wishing things were different), you can "dance with life," in the words of meditation teacher Phillip Moffitt (Moffitt 2008). Mindfulness, then, leads directly to liberation—to freedom from clinging and an end to the afflictions of greed, aversion, and ignorance.

A Buddhist Understanding of Habits and Ways to Transform Them

The Buddha taught that a key determinant of our happiness and well-being is how we meet the present moment. If we meet the present moment by trying to hold on to pleasant experiences and avoid or escape unpleasant experiences, or trying to distract ourselves from neutral or "boring" experiences, we'll suffer. Not only that, but a preoccupation with avoiding unpleasant, neutral, or "boring" experiences will naturally keep such experiences in the forefront of our minds.

As the Buddha said, "Whatever a *bhikkhu* [monk, or practitioner] frequently thinks and ponders upon, that will become the inclination of his mind" (Bodhi 1995, 208).

Also, the more we repeat thoughts and actions, the more likely we are to keep repeating them. It's easier to think and do things that you've thought and done before, even if those thoughts and actions lead to suffering. Thus every thought you have and every action you do that leads to suffering keeps you on the road to suffering, making it harder to live according to your intentions and goals. If you think angry, jealous, or cruel thoughts, you incline your mind in that direction, sowing seeds of future afflictive thoughts and actions. But every time you go against your habits or make a mindful choice, you'll find it a little easier to do the same thing again in the future. If you think a kind thought or carry out a generous action, you incline your mind in that direction, sowing seeds of future positive and kind thoughts and actions.

This is the meaning of *karma*: you reap what you sow. It might sound deterministic, except that you can break the cycle through mindfulness. However heavily the past weighs on the present, you have the potential to end the cycle here and now by saying yes to whatever is present, including painful bodily sensations, intense emotions, and insistent thoughts and urges. Many of the Buddha's teachings—such as focusing your mind, cultivating wise intentions, and practicing loving-kindness—are methods, or skillful means, of helping you be open to what is.

Mindfulness is a key to ending unhealthy or harmful habits, because the practice of mindfulness addresses the underlying urges and triggers of habitual behaviors. What's more, mindfulness offers ways of being open to your urges, experiencing their impermanence, and letting them arise and pass without clinging or resistance.

Mindfulness and Changing the Brain—Neuroplasticity

In the past two decades, scientists have made great advances in understanding the human brain. Though it used to be thought that our brains essentially stopped developing once we reached adulthood, we now know that our brains change throughout our lives. In other words, what we do and how we use our attention changes our brains and can make an enormous difference in our lives. Mindfulness training has been shown to have a significant impact in this regard, including bringing about positive physical changes to the brain.

A 2011 study showed that the practice of mindfulness was associated with certain changes in the brain. Among participants in an eight-week mindfulness meditation program, the density of neurons and other cells in areas of the brain linked to self-awareness, compassion, and introspection *increased*; in addition, the density of neurons and other cells in an area of the brain associated with stress and anxiety *decreased*. These changes in participants' brains were the result of spending an average of only twenty-seven minutes a day in meditation practice over the eight-week period (Hölzel et al. 2011).

The potential for improving your neural structure through what you do and how you pay attention will be particularly important in helping you balance out your brain's negative tendencies.

Your Brain's Negative Bias

The brain you have inherited is the product of tens of millions of years of evolution. It's an extraordinarily complex organ capable of great wonders, but it can also get you in trouble, if you're not paying attention.

Your brain and nervous system are primed to focus on the negative—on what could kill or harm you. This focus on threats helped your ancestors survive and pass on their genes, and this defensive faculty of the brain has been called the "survival brain." From a survival standpoint, it's more beneficial to be hypervigilant about imminent dangers and comparatively less concerned about achieving positive goals, which can wait until the threat has passed. Thus, your brain pays much more attention to negative stimuli and experiences than positive ones. For example, if one person says something positive about you and another person says something negative about you, which remark do you tend to obsess about?

Neuropsychologist and meditation teacher Rick Hanson has described the brain's bias as like "Velcro for negative experiences and Teflon for positive ones," so that overcoming the effects of a single negative interaction typically requires no less than five positive interactions (Hanson 2009, 41). Think of the price you pay for your "survival brain's" negative bias when your stress response becomes activated in reaction to a potential challenge: Stress hormones (including cortisol, the primary stress hormone) are released. Blood is pumped to your arm and leg muscles to help you fight or run. Bodily functions that aren't essential to your immediate survival, such as those associated with digestion and reproduction, are shut down. Continuously thinking about a potential challenge can keep you locked in this state of stress and anxiety in which you're ready to respond to perceived threats. And this, in turn, can trigger unhealthy habitual responses that you resort to for comfort or relief.

Difficult emotions, such as anger, shame, and sadness, which enable you to respond to threatening or painful situations in the way described above, can also get you into trouble. This happens when, instead of treating your emotions as signals containing useful information, you identify with them and continually revisit them.

The good news is that, through practices of mindful awareness, you can take advantage of your brain's capacity to change. You can, as Rick Hanson encourages, balance the negative bias of the brain by "taking in the good"—consciously cultivating and appreciating emotions that are conducive to well-being, such as gratitude, joy, love, and compassion (Hanson 2009, 67). And you can train your mind, through mindfulness practices, to experience all of your mind states and feelings—including the sensations, urges, and cravings associated with habits—as impermanent and impersonal. You can stop letting them define you. This will allow you to make choices and respond in ways that truly serve you.

How Mindfulness Works

The renowned Zen Buddhist teacher, poet, and peace activist Thich Nhat Hanh titled one of his books *The Miracle of Mindfulness* (Nhat Hanh 1975). The "miracle" lies in the transformation that comes from being willing to meet your experience without resistance, without struggle, and with an open and accepting heart. What seems painful, scary, or too much to endure can become a path to growth and healing when met wholeheartedly. As spiritual teacher Eckhart Tolle said, "Whatever you accept completely, you go beyond" (Tolle 2003).

When you resist or avoid any part of your experience, it's as though you put a psychic wall around it. Paraphrasing Franklin D. Roosevelt's famous statement, you live in fear of the fear itself. When you avoid an experience, a feeling, or an emotion, that experience, feeling, or emotion doesn't go away; rather, it's fueled by your resistance, ready to return when conditions are appropriate. *What you resist persists.*

It's the willingness to be fully open to an experience that allows it to "self-liberate," a term from Tibetan Buddhism; without the fuel of resistance, without struggle, any feelings come and go. The path to freedom from suffering is, ironically, willingness to experience suffering. The challenge is to have the courage to meet your pain and your suffering without either identifying with it or resisting it.

Mindfulness is simple in that you need only "be here now"—be open to your experience just as it is. That includes the sights and sounds around you, as well as your sensations, your emotions, and your thoughts.

But mindfulness isn't easy, because there's so much that can pull you away from the present moment. You may be used to spending much of your time lost in ruminating about the past, comparing yourself to others, or worrying about the future (we'll discuss this in chapter 6). You may have had painful or traumatic experiences that have left a legacy of vigilance and fear that, if not addressed, make it difficult to be fully present. Ironically, the technological advances that enable you to be in constant communication with others and access information instantly tend to separate you from the world around you and can distance you from the people right next to you. And finally, through advertising and other tactics, you have been primed to want things you don't have. For example, as Michael Moss has noted, "There is nothing accidental in the grocery store…the gentle canned music; the in-store bakery aromas; the soft-drink coolers by the check-out lanes" (Moss 2014, 346–47). Companies spend billions of dollars to spur consumer spending habits and perpetuate a sense of wanting. This wanting can make it hard to simply notice your surroundings without wanting something you don't have or wishing things were different, whether you're at home or out and about.

So, being mindful isn't easy; it takes practice to be present. But when you're mindful of your moment-to-moment experience, you'll cultivate a variety of skills that recent studies show affect different parts of the brain and thus contribute to physical, emotional, mental, and spiritual benefits and changes.

Contemporary scientific research into mindfulness is helping clarify how mindfulness works and how particular aspects of mindfulness training may lead to specific outcomes. Mindfulness may help different people in different ways. For example, it may help people with attention-deficit/hyperactivity disorder improve their focus, it may help people with addictions tolerate their cravings, and it may help people with psychological disorders experience negative feelings without being overwhelmed by them.

How Mindfulness Can Help You Change Unwanted Habits

The practice of mindfulness has been shown to be a highly effective approach for alleviating stress, anxiety, and depression, as well as a host of other conditions. Applying mindfulness to harmful or unhelpful habits offers similar potential. Mindfulness brings stimuli, urges, or cravings—and the habitual behaviors they trigger—into your conscious awareness. For 2,500 years, meditators have practiced mindfulness as a path to letting go of painful, afflictive, and habitual mind states and emotions. This history is now supported by a growing body of scientific research that points to the ways in which mindfulness can be a key to habit change.

Studies on applying mindfulness to habitual behaviors, including addictions, have shown great promise. In a smoking-cessation study, 36 percent of participants who received training in mindfulness had quit smoking at the end of a four-week program, compared with 15 percent of participants who received standard smoking-cessation training. The abstinence rates at the seventeen-week follow-up were 31 percent for those who received training in mindfulness, versus 6 percent for those who received standard smoking-cessation training (Brewer et al. 2011).

A study of inmates in a correctional facility showed that those who took a *vipassana* ("insight" or mindfulness) meditation program reduced their substance use, as well as had fewer alcohol-related problems and diminished psychiatric symptoms (Adams et al. 2014).

The changes brought about by mindfulness can have wide-ranging positive effects, as the following case study illustrates.

Thomas's Story

Thomas had practiced meditation on and off for many years. As his aging mother's health deteriorated and she developed dementia, his mindfulness practice kept him, in his words, "sane and relatively compassionate."

After his mother's death, Thomas felt a surge of psychic, physical, and creative energy. But he also had fallen into some unhealthy habits of procrastination, distraction, and impulsivity. He wanted to write, but he found himself doing anything but sitting down to write.

Thomas came to a six-week class that I was teaching on harnessing the power of mindfulness to support habit change. Two things helped him make a shift that led to real change in his life: First, his earlier training in mindfulness had taught him to practice in a particular way and assume a certain posture while meditating. The different approach presented in the class, that of "find what works for *you*," opened space for Thomas to make changes in his posture that allowed him to sit in a way that was comfortable and relaxed. As he shared with me, "For decades, discomfort while meditating had meant that the practice had rarely been fruitful, had generated an ongoing sense of failure, and rather than becoming a self-reinforcing habit, had remained an unappealing chore. Once I found a posture that worked, I found myself sitting more and more, enjoying simply being there in the silence, 'just sitting.'"

Second, while meditating, Thomas had been unable to let go of concerns about how long he had been sitting and how much time remained in his period of meditation. A chance conversation with a fellow student led him to download a meditation app that allowed him to begin and end his meditations with the pleasant sound of a bell, freeing him from his preoccupation with time. It also established a kind of electronic accountability (by tracking how long he meditated each day and providing information on others who were meditating at the same time).

For the first time in over thirty years, Thomas began meditating consistently for twenty to forty minutes a day. He shared how he had a greater sense of calm overall: "My mood is lighter. I respond to setbacks more quickly. Humor is nearer at hand. But the most palpable outgrowth of the daily meditation practice has been greater consistency with regard to physical exercise, with thirty minutes or more of yoga a day. One positive habit seems to emerge from the other, along with commitment in one area fostering greater commitment in the other."

Thomas shared that the positive shift in his meditation practice influenced just about every area of his life. "Eating mindfully, I am aware of feelings of fullness, and, as a result, eat a bit less and enjoy it more. I am noticing my own actions more, aware of my surroundings, less lost in thought, and less likely to abandon tasks before completing them."

Researchers (for example, Gardner, Lally, and Wardle 2012) also have noted this "positive domino effect": one healthy habit can trigger other healthy behaviors, even where there's no obvious or direct connection between them. For example, someone who starts exercising may begin to eat more healthily without consciously deciding to do so. Thomas summarized how this dynamic affected his life: "Greater energy has fostered even more energy. Increased hope and optimism have fostered more vivid and enlivening optimism. Mindful alertness in some areas of my life (for example, awareness of sounds, visual details, and tactile feelings) has led to more awakened consciousness in many other areas—with respect to world events and the natural world."

Different kinds of habits have different feelings and energies associated with them, but all can be experienced and changed when met with a kind, interested, and accepting awareness. In the chapters to come, we'll explore and work with four main kinds of habits:

1. Habits of *wanting*, including craving or habitually seeking food, drink, drugs, sex, or any other object of desire

2. Habits of *distraction*—moving away from your present-moment experience toward something that seems more attractive, interesting, or exciting, such as social media, text messages, e-mail, or TV

3. Habits of *resistance*—wanting to avoid something you find unpleasant or painful. (Anger, frustration, judgment, and impatience often signal that you're resisting.)

4. Habits of *doing, stress, and worry*—feeling as if you're always on your way somewhere, without enough time to get everything done; or always checking items off a "to-do" list, with a stressed, often frenetic sense of disconnection from the present

Whether you engage in mostly one type of habit or all of them, mindfulness can connect you with your deepest intentions, shine a light on behaviors that don't serve you, and help support your intention to make changes.

The mindfulness practices to come will help you bring awareness to your habit urges at three distinct times—before they arise, while you're experiencing them, and after they have passed. The practices will also nurture attitudes of kindness, acceptance, and curiosity, which are conducive to habit change. Finally, the practices will provide skillful ways of relating to challenging emotions and mind states, so that you can safely experience the emotions and mind states your habitual behavior helps you avoid. This will help loosen your identification with thoughts and beliefs that fuel unhealthy habits.

A key element of mindfulness as a path to habit change is that mindfulness helps you get to the *root* of the habit, beneath the behavior itself. As a friend and colleague of mine discovered, it's easy to replace one unhealthy habit with another. "I stopped drinking in the evening, but I often wind up craving some food 'reward' for not drinking," she said. "Even though the food is healthy, it's still too much. To distract me from that craving, I started playing games on my computer as a way to make time pass before I was tired enough to go to bed. That keeps me from having to be with my feelings. But being on my computer late in the evening affects my sleeping. It made me realize I'm exchanging one unhealthy habit for something not quite as bad, but still something that distracts my attention." Her experience opened her eyes to the importance of going to the source of the habit pattern: "When I saw this pattern, I realized that if I don't open to the underlying energy of *wanting this moment to be different*, my suffering will continue, but in a new form."

Seven Skillful Mindfulness Practices to Transform Habits

In this book, you'll discover for yourself how mindfulness supports changing unwanted or harmful habits and/or cultivating more healthy and helpful ones, through the following seven practical skills:

1. Learning to identify unhealthy or unwanted habits, seeing how they're not serving your needs, and consciously establishing an intention to change and a course of action to effect change

This skill will help you connect with your deepest wishes for yourself, see the harm caused by unhealthy habits, and bring your actions into alignment with your intentions.

2. Relaxing, being open to your experience, and welcoming the good, the bad, and the ugly aspects of that experience

    Cultivating a relaxed and nonjudging awareness in your body, heart, and mind will help you simply feel the cravings and challenging emotions that—if pushed away or, alternatively, allowed to take over—can lead to unhealthy or unwanted behaviors.

3. Cultivating attitudes and qualities that support mindfulness, particularly attitudes of kindness, curiosity, and acceptance

    When you bring these attitudes to your established habits, you'll simply acknowledge your behaviors and thoughts as they are without making them "wrong" or "bad," and you'll avoid adding judgment and harsh criticism to habitual behaviors, which often perpetuates and reinforces them.

4. Focusing your attention through mindfulness of breathing (or of another object of meditation) and learning to return to your breath when you find yourself on autopilot or lost in thought

    Developing focus and concentration will help counter your mind's tendency to go on autopilot and into habitual patterns of thought—and returning nonjudgmentally to your object of meditation will help create new, healthier patterns.

5. Bringing awareness to the thoughts and beliefs that often underlie established habits

   This skill will loosen the grip of the often deep-seated beliefs and narratives that can undergird habitual patterns of thought and action, and it'll allow you to accept your thoughts without identifying with or getting swept up in them.

6. Learning to "ride the waves" of difficult experiences and developing the capacity to stay present with challenging bodily sensations, emotions, and mind states

   This skill will help you learn that you can be open to unpleasant or difficult experiences without getting pulled into unhealthy or unwanted behaviors.

7. Developing beneficial states of heart and mind—particularly loving-kindness and self-compassion—that will help you create space for difficult or painful experiences

   This skill is essential for working with challenging experiences—it'll help you make room for painful experiences and develop the skills and capacity to deal kindly and wisely with challenging emotions and mind states.

A caveat: Although mindfulness can be helpful in any situation, mindfulness or specific meditation practices may not always be the best place to start. There may be times when being present with what you're feeling is too much to bear. For example, if you're experiencing a panic attack, rather than sitting still and bringing awareness to your breath, it may be better to take a walk or to talk with a trusted friend or health professional. To be able to meet pain or challenging emotions with kindness, you need a certain degree of stability and resilience. The practices provided in this book will help you calm your body and mind, but you're the best judge of whether a particular practice or approach will be useful to you at any given time. Mindfulness will be a great support in developing and cultivating this kind of discernment.

Also, keep in mind that mindfulness is not a magic formula that immediately transforms long-established patterns. It's a training and a practice that, over time, leads to change through awareness and conscious choice. And it may be only one of several complementary approaches to working with complex conditions or patterns. For example, in the case of trauma or addictions, mindfulness can complement and enhance the effectiveness of therapy, medication, 12-step programs, and other approaches.

Practice 2: SOBER Breathing Space

This mindfulness practice, taken from mindfulness-based cognitive therapy (MBCT), is one that you can do almost anywhere. It can be particularly helpful whenever someone or something triggers you to respond in a reactive way or whenever you're anxious or stressed and feel the urge to soothe yourself with food, drink, drugs, tobacco, or some other unhealthy habit. All you need to do is remember the acronym SOBER, which stands for Stop, Observe, Breathe, Expand Awareness, and Respond Mindfully.

1. **S**top. Slow down, and bring awareness to your mind and body in this moment.

    Let's say you have just had a difficult encounter with a coworker, in which you both got angry and defensive. When you stop and bring awareness to your experience, you might notice that your body is tense, your face is flushed, and your thoughts are racing.

2. Observe what's happening in your body, emotions, and thoughts with acceptance and without judgment.

    If you're feeling angry, allow yourself to feel the tightness in your chest and the heat in your face. You may experience some relaxation as you do so. Notice the thoughts that come up, without latching onto them.

3. Breathe. Take a few deeper breaths and then focus simply on the sensations of breathing. Allow yourself to feel your breath as you breathe in and out, perhaps feeling some release as you exhale.

4. Expand your awareness to include your whole body and the overall situation and context with a kind and accepting attention. Let yourself take in the feelings, thoughts, and emotions that are present, with acceptance.

5. Respond mindfully—make a choice to respond in a way that supports your deepest intentions. Whatever is happening in your mind and body, know that you have a choice in how you respond.

(Adapted from Bowen, Chawla, and Marlatt 2011, 90)

The Basics of Mindfulness—Summing Up

Being mindful means intentionally paying attention to your moment-to-moment experience with acceptance and without judgment. Mindfulness is a universal human quality of awareness that is present in all major religious traditions, as well as many secular practices. It has been most fully developed and investigated in Buddhist teachings, as a direct path to freedom from suffering. Much of the current interest in mindfulness comes from the adaptation of Buddhist teachings and practices to a secular context—for example, in mindfulness-based stress reduction (MBSR)—and from the research studies that have shown the benefits of mindfulness.

Mindfulness is a simple practice of being open to your experience just as it is, here and now. Yet it's not easy, because there's much in our evolution, culture, conditioning, and habits that takes us away from our present experience. For example, the focus of our "survival brain" on defending against perceived threats can generate unhealthy patterns and habits that lead to stress and suffering.

The good news—as both ancient wisdom and modern neuroscience demonstrate—is that the practice of cultivating awareness with kindness and acceptance supports greater well-being and a lessening of stress and anxiety.

Mindfulness is a key to changing unhealthy habits and developing more positive and helpful ones. In bringing awareness to what you're largely unconscious of, you can make the invisible visible. This involves bringing awareness to patterns of thought and action that have become automatic and unconscious through repetition.

A series of essential skills and practices designed to help you change unhealthy habits and develop more helpful ones are laid out in the chapters ahead.

PART 2

PUTTING WISDOM INTO PRACTICE

CHAPTER 3

The Power of Intention: What Matters Most?

If you don't know where you are going, you'll end up someplace else.

—Attributed to Yogi Berra

A ll the great transformative advances in our world—from ending slavery and segregation to traveling to outer space—began with an understanding either that something was wrong and needed to be changed or that there were new possibilities waiting to be explored. Next came the intention to make a change.

If you look at your own life, you can probably think of important changes you have made—perhaps to live in a more healthy way, or to be more kind and thoughtful in intimate relationships. You may recall realizing that your old ways weren't serving you. And so you set an intention to make a change, and then put that intention into action.

Intention is the inner compass that sets you on your journey. Without clear intentions you'll drift, acting out old habits, like flotsam swept on the water. You'll be carried along by thought patterns and behavioral patterns that may have become so familiar that they seem as much a part of who you are as the color of your eyes or hair. You'll become so accustomed to identifying with your anger or worries that you'll think, *I'm an angry or fearful person.* You may even believe it's not possible to change these patterns.

Clear intentions are essential to bringing about meaningful change. As you learned in chapter 1, because habits operate through fast-moving brain processes, you may respond automatically to certain events, even when you intend to act in a different way. In order to change entrenched habits, you need to develop strong and clear intentions that connect your moment-by-moment actions with your deepest values.

How to Set an Intention

It's helpful to take a three-step approach to setting your intentions:

1. Clarify and connect with what matters most in your life—and commit to these deepest aspirations.

2. Identify the habits that prevent you from living out your deepest intentions—and commit to take action to change these habits.

3. Align your thoughts and actions moment-by-moment with your deepest intentions by asking yourself: *Does this thought/action/response serve happiness? Does it support my deepest aspirations?*

Let's walk through each of these steps.

Connect with What Matters Most

To transform unhealthy thought patterns and behavioral patterns, start by connecting with your deepest intentions and values. When I ask myself, *What matters most to me in life?* the answer is peace and loving relationships. When I ask myself, *What's my deepest longing for myself and the world?* the answer is a more compassionate world. What comes to mind when you ask yourself these same questions? There are no right answers, but at times you may be satisfied with less than you deserve. For example, if your deepest wish is for more money or a job you like, ask yourself whether these wishes point to a deeper aspiration.

When you have decided what it is you want—when you can express what matters most to you—visualize yourself fully embodying this wish for yourself. Let yourself experience the emotions, sensations, and feelings of living this intention. How does it feel in your body, heart, and mind? Close your eyes, and as you breathe in, reflect on your intention, using a word or phrase, if it's helpful, such as "peace," "happiness," "love," or "an awake life." Write down your intention, and revisit it regularly. You may wish to begin each day with a reflection on your deepest intention and your aspiration for the day. You can also use ordinary experiences throughout your day as reminders to pause and remember what matters most to you. For example, whenever you're driving and you come to a red light, rather than waiting impatiently or checking your phone, you can take a couple of full breaths and reflect on the intention you want to embody.

Recognize What's Getting in Your Way

Next, think about thought patterns and behavioral patterns that may hinder your realization of your deepest intentions. Is there an activity, such as being so consumed by work that you have little time for your family, that keeps you disconnected from yourself or your loved ones? Do negative self-judgments or thoughts of unworthiness prevent you from believing that meaningful change is possible? When you think about these patterns, how do you feel? What bodily sensations, emotions, and thoughts are present? You might notice tension in your belly or chest or tightness in your breathing. If you do, try to meet these sensations with kindness, interest, and acceptance, letting them come and go in their own time.

Sometimes the habits that prevent you from getting closer to what matters most may not be dramatic or very obvious but still cause stress, dissatisfaction, suffering, or a feeling of not being fully connected to yourself.

A number of years ago, I had a habit of drinking a couple of glasses of wine at home each evening after work. It seemed relatively innocuous. The wine wasn't burning a big hole in my budget, and the few drinks didn't seem like a "problem." But as I paid closer attention, I felt a kind of "leaning in" to the drinking in the evening. I would look forward to it as a release after a full day. And there was also some anxiety—as I left work, I would wonder: *Do I have a bottle of wine at home? Do I need to stop to buy one?* I also had the feeling that an evening without a glass or two of wine would be less pleasant, that I would be missing something I enjoyed.

The sense of anxiety accompanied by some bodily tension pointed to the need to pay attention. There was a feeling of unease, and some clinging—the first two of the Buddha's

Four Noble Truths (suffering, and clinging as the cause of suffering).

Over time, with intention and attention—and initially some discomfort at not having my regular habit to lean on—I ended the habit of drinking in the evening. I would have a beer or glass of wine only occasionally, and out of conscious choice rather than mindlessly or out of habit. Looking back, I believe that what I gave up wasn't the wine as much as the wanting—the feeling that I needed to have a couple of glasses of wine to feel relaxed and at ease in the evening. The change in the habit brought me a sense of ease, as if I had put down a burden I had been carrying. I felt more at peace in the absence of the habitual wanting to drink in the evening.

What stops you from feeling fully alive and connected to your deepest intentions?

Connect with Your Intentions Moment to Moment

Each of your voluntary actions is preceded by an intention. Often, however, you may not be aware of your intentions when acting mindlessly or out of habit: You scratch an itch without being aware of the intention that preceded the movement to scratch. You say something as a reflex or reaction, unaware of the potential impact of your words. You find you have gone to the freezer and eaten a half pint of ice cream without ever having made a conscious choice.

What you experience in any moment is the fruit of past intentions and actions, as well as external factors. Whatever is present is *here*; you can't change what's here now, be it a feeling of excitement, a headache, a sad mood, or a sense of peace. But you can choose how you respond to what's here and sow the seeds of future well-being—or, alternatively, sow the seeds of suffering—by how you meet this moment. If you meet this moment with presence, with mindfulness, you'll cultivate future happiness and well-being. And if your deepest intention is peace, you can bring peace to this moment. Dorothy Hunt expresses this quality of presence in her poem "Peace Is This Moment Without Judgment":

> Do you think peace requires an end to war?
> Or tigers eating only vegetables?
> Does peace require an absence from
> your boss, your spouse, yourself?...
> Do you think peace will come some other place than
>   here?
> Some other time than Now?
> In some other heart than yours?
>
> Peace is this moment without judgment.
> That is all. This moment in the Heart-space
> where everything that is is welcome.
> Peace is this moment without thinking
> that it should be some other way,
> that you should feel some other thing,
> that your life should unfold according to your plans.
>
> Peace is this moment without judgment,
> this moment in the heart-space where
> everything that is is welcome.
>
> (Hunt, n.d.)

In this, or any, moment, what action or response serves your deepest intention and can help you abandon an unhealthy habit or cultivate a more helpful one?

Intention—the Buddha's Quest

In chapter 2, I described key elements in the life of the Buddha. Siddhartha's journey to becoming the Buddha provides one of the clearest and most inspiring examples of the power of intention.

All of his actions—leaving home, becoming a wandering mendicant, studying under well-known teachers, practicing rigorous austerities—were aimed at answering the question "Is freedom possible?" His studies did not resolve the question, and his ascetic practices only reinforced an inner duality. But he learned from those experiences and continued his search with diligence. Sitting in meditation under a tree in northern India, he realized that freedom comes not from outside of us but from letting go of clinging to anything. Henceforth, he was known as the Buddha, one who through his own intention and effort has realized the end of suffering.

Practice 3: Cultivating Intention in Working with Habits

Over the next week, take some time each day to reflect on what matters most to you in your life—your deepest wish for yourself, your life, and the world. Write down your intentions, and find times to reflect on them during the day.

Here are two practices to help bring your actions into alignment with your intentions. If you like, you can do them as guided meditations using the audio tracks available for download at the publisher's website: http://www.newharbinger.com/32370.

Bringing Awareness to Habits That Hinder Peace and Happiness

As you go through your day, notice whenever a situation, a person, a news story, a world event, or anything else triggers you to think or act in a way that's out of alignment with your deepest intentions or values. Are there any similarities in the kinds of situations you find challenging, or when you behave in ways that you would prefer not to? For some people, watching cable television news leaves them feeling angry or righteous or judgmental. For others, having to wait for something spurs feelings of impatience or frustration. And for some, feelings of stress or anxiety generate a desire to eat, drink, smoke, shop, or engage in other habitual behaviors to alleviate the uncomfortable feelings.

What are the typical ways in which you respond to the urges or triggers you experience? When faced with a difficult situation, emotion, or decision, do you get caught up in thoughts that seem to seize control of your mind—for example, anxious, fearful, angry, or judgmental thoughts? Or do you procrastinate, "space out," go online, or watch TV? When you have negative, painful, or difficult feelings, it's natural to want comfort or relief. Do you seek comfort in food, drink, sex, work, or some other mode of self-soothing?

Choose one of these patterns of responding, and become as familiar as you can with the sensations, emotions, thoughts, and beliefs linked to it.

- **Sensations:** First, what do you notice in your body when you feel compelled to respond in this way? It can be helpful to name what you're aware of—"tightness in my chest," "shallow breathing," "muscles tightening," "wanting to move, do something." Simply be aware of these feelings and meet them without judgment.

- **Emotions:** Next, what emotions or mind states do you experience when you feel triggered to respond in this way? Name them, if it's helpful—"worry," "judgment," "anger," "frustration," "wanting," "boredom." Notice how these emotions or states of mind feel in your body. Notice the thoughts that accompany them, and allow them to arise, meeting them with kindness and acceptance.

- **Thoughts and beliefs:** Finally, what thought, belief, or story arises when you feel the urge to respond in this way? Try to untangle the thought from the bodily sensations and emotions. It might be *This feeling is overwhelming; I've got to have x,* or *I'll feel much better if I have y,* or *If I don't keep working/planning/moving, then something really bad will happen.* Meet this thought or belief with kindness and acceptance. If you can note the thought, bow to it (metaphorically), and let it go, it'll begin to lose its power over you.

Cultivating a New, Healthier Habit

Reflect on your deepest intentions and how developing a new goal, such as losing weight or exercising regularly, supports this intention.

1. Make a *specific plan* to achieve this goal or cultivate this new habit. What will you do? When? How? Where? For example, if your goal is to lose weight by avoiding unhealthy food, eating more nutritious food, and exercising regularly, think of the specific steps and activities that will help you achieve this goal. For example:

   - I'll make a list before I go shopping and only include healthful foods, and I'll commit to buying only what's on the list and not purchasing anything on impulse.

   - Each day when I return from work, I'll feed the cat, then put on my sneakers and take a thirty-minute walk through the neighborhood or in the park.

- I'll bring healthy snacks to work each day so that when I feel the urge to eat, I won't get a candy bar from the vending machine.

2. *Visualize* how you'll feel when you're carrying out the healthy behavior. What do you see, hear, smell, taste, feel, and think when you imagine yourself engaging in this activity that aligns with your intentions? Allow yourself to take in these feelings, sensations, images, and thoughts. Studies (for example, Morris, Spittle, and Watt 2005) show that when we visualize ourselves carrying out a particular action, we activate the same areas of the brain as when we're actually engaged in the activity. For example, imagining themselves getting the ball in the basket helps basketball players create new pathways in the brain.

3. Imagine in as much detail as possible a potential *obstacle* to carrying out this new healthier behavior, and imagine how you'll overcome this challenge, if and when it arises. For example, if your goal is to lose weight by eating more healthfully, an obstacle might be walking down a particular aisle in the supermarket and seeing your favorite sweets. Visualize yourself meeting this obstacle by choosing to avoid that aisle or by bringing awareness to your breath and body as you walk down that aisle, then moving on.

Stanford University psychologist Kelly McGonigal suggests six useful questions for cultivating a new habit and meeting a goal you have set:

1. What's my most important goal?

2. What's my deepest motivation for realizing this goal?

3. What specific action can I take to honor this motivation?

4. When, where, and how am I willing to take this action?

5. What's the biggest obstacle to taking this action?

6. What action will I take to prevent or overcome this obstacle? (McGonigal 2012)

The Power of Intention: What Matters Most?—Summing Up

If you wish to change unhealthy or unwanted habits, your intentions are key. Unless you're clear about why you want to make a change in your life and how making a change will align you with your deepest aspirations, your old thought patterns and behavioral patterns will prevail.

In order to change deeply entrenched habits, you need to be clear about what matters most to you and about the thought patterns and behavioral patterns that present obstacles to your deepest aspirations, then commit to taking action to initiate change.

Three steps can help you change unhealthy habits:

1. Think about what matters most in your life, and identify your deepest intention. Commit to aligning your actions and your life with that intention.

2. Identify the habits that get in the way of what matters most, and commit to the intention to make a change—bringing mindfulness to changing an old habit or cultivating a new, more helpful one.

3. As you bring awareness to your moment-to-moment experience, establish—and return to—the intention to move toward your deepest aspiration. Choose to stay with your present-moment experience, rather than defaulting to habitual thoughts and actions.

CHAPTER 4

Welcoming Your "Guests"

"Clearing"

Do not try to save
the whole world
or do anything grandiose.
Instead, create
a clearing
in the dense forest
of your life
and wait there
patiently,
until the song
that is yours alone to sing
falls into your open cupped hands
and you recognize and greet it.
Only then will you know
how to give yourself
to this world,
so worthy of rescue.

—Martha Postlethwaite

When you act in a way that's out of alignment with your deepest values and aspirations, you'll experience stress and suffering. When you do something you know is unhealthy, such as eating unconsciously or losing yourself in the wasteland of electronic distractions, you'll feel a gap between what you're doing and how you want to live—and that's painful. Add self-criticism and self-judgment, and you may even believe you're a flawed or bad person because of your actions.

There's a story of a man who wanted to go to Newcastle and asked someone how to get there. The person responded, "If I wanted to go to Newcastle, I wouldn't start from here."

Often we wish we could start from somewhere else. If only we had the Dalai Lama's equanimity or Nelson Mandela's forgiveness or Mother Teresa's compassion, it would be so much easier to be peaceful, forgiving, or kind. But if we want to know peace and freedom in our lives, we have no choice but to start from where we are.

As you learned in chapter 2, the first of the Four Noble Truths teaches the importance of acknowledging your suffering. This recognition is essential if you're to find a way out. Similarly, acknowledging your harmful or unwanted habits by bringing awareness to them is the first step to changing them.

The move from thinking *This shouldn't be happening* to recognizing that *This is true (and painful)* can bring profound insight and is an important step toward greater freedom.

But changing your habits is challenging. To create new thought patterns and behavioral patterns, you need to first notice your triggers, the things that encourage you to act out. Once you learn to notice your triggers, you'll have two choices any time you feel the urge to engage in a habit:

- One is to carry out the habitual behavior.

- The other is to let yourself experience the feelings, sensations, thoughts, and emotions that are present, then choose not to carry out the habitual behavior.

This latter choice may not lead to any external action, but may simply involve tuning in to your experience and letting the impulse pass in its own time. Or, it may involve choosing a healthier response, such as replacing a walk to the donut shop with a walk in the park. In this way, you'll create a new thought pattern or behavioral pattern that's in alignment with your values and intentions.

A helpful question to ask yourself when you feel the urge to act out an unhealthy habit is *What would I have to experience if I were not to eat this cookie or smoke this cigarette? What would I have to feel?*

Training in mindfulness begins with opening to your experience as it is. But, mindfulness is much more than a technique for cultivating awareness of your experience. It's an attitude of relating fully, with an open heart, to life as it is— recognizing what you're experiencing and meeting it with kindness and acceptance.

The willingness to inhabit your feelings—to feel sadness without escaping into distraction by checking e-mail, to experience a craving without resorting to short-term relief by lighting a cigarette—is what will allow you to change an unwanted habit.

This willingness will help you see that all experiences, however difficult, are temporary. In addition, it'll help you see that the things you experience ultimately don't define you. If you can let yourself feel pain and sadness and shame without telling yourself that these difficult emotions and sensations mean something about you, you can simply experience them and let them go, like weather systems passing through and moving on.

Cultivating a welcoming attitude, saying yes to what is, is key to changing unhealthy habits. The thirteenth-century Sufi poet Maulana Jalāl al-Din Rumi captures this welcoming attitude in his poem "The Guest House":

This being human is a guest-house
Every morning a new arrival.

A joy, a depression, a meanness,
some momentary awareness comes
as an unexpected visitor.

Welcome and entertain them all!
Even if they're a crowd of sorrows,
who violently sweep your house
empty of its furniture,
still treat each guest honorably.
He may be clearing you
out for some new delight.

The dark thought, the shame, the malice,
meet them at the door laughing,
and invite them in.

Be grateful for whoever comes,
Because each has been sent
as a guide from beyond.

(Jalāl al-Din Rumi 2004, 109)

When you welcome your experience in this way, you'll take refuge in the truth. You'll no longer struggle with your experience, or with life. Anthony de Mello, the Jesuit writer and philosopher, said freedom or enlightenment is "absolute cooperation with the inevitable" (cited in Adyashanti 2008, 157). In other words, although you might have wished this moment to be different, *this* is how things are right now. To fight with this truth is to suffer. To be open to this moment—this feeling, sensation, mood, emotion, or thought—without judgment or resistance is a doorway to freedom and a path to ending unwanted habits.

Martha's Story

Martha, a member of my weekly meditation class, was caught in a traffic jam on her way to work. She had a busy and difficult workday ahead, with back-to-back meetings and some challenging talks with staff members. She felt nervous and anxious. Without even being conscious of her intention, she felt her hands moving toward her phone to check her e-mail. But her practice of mindfulness allowed her to pause. She brought awareness to the urge to check her messages and paid attention to her bodily sensations and emotions—the tightness in her stomach; a restless, confined, and anxious feeling that the distraction of her phone might soothe—and she chose to stay with the feelings. They weren't pleasant, but she noticed that they didn't last long. Her mind moved to thoughts about the day ahead at work, but she chose to come back to her bodily sensations and her breath. She breathed into the feelings and felt the waves of sensation come and go.

In the process, Martha relaxed. She was stuck in traffic, but nothing was wrong. She was warm and comfortable in her car. She was going nowhere fast, but once she accepted that this was the reality, she realized it didn't need to be a source of suffering. The rest of the day was the future and could be dealt with in its own time. She looked over at the driver in the next lane. He was busy texting. She laughed—not at him but at the way our human minds can lead us to peace or, alternatively, to stress and worry. "I know I'll forget this insight sometimes, but I'm so grateful to know that I can always come back to the present moment, knowing there's freedom here and now when I let go of the stories and of the future," she said later.

Relaxing Your Body and Mind

When you open yourself fully to your experience, life will become much less problematic. Whatever arises, you can meet it with equanimity. Challenging, difficult, or painful experiences won't stop being challenging, difficult, or painful, but you can meet them as a challenge rather than as a curse—as something that shouldn't be happening.

The realization that your freedom and your peace depend more on how you meet and respond to your experience than on what happens to you is a profound insight of spiritual life. Viktor Frankl, the renowned psychologist who survived the Nazi concentration camps, expressed how even in the most extreme situations we have the freedom to determine how we respond:

We who lived in concentration camps can remember the men who walked through the huts comforting others, giving away their last piece of bread. They may have been few in number, but they offer sufficient proof that everything can be taken from a man but one thing: the last of the human freedoms—to choose one's attitude in any given set of circumstances, to choose one's own way. (Frankl 2006, 86–87)

But to come to this realization without the catalyst of an extremely traumatic experience is a journey, a training in meeting your experience courageously, welcoming the guests.

The "guests," however, are often tempestuous, rowdy, and insistent. The message from your "survival brain" to your nervous system may be to run, fight, or freeze. And a counter-vailing message from your prefrontal cortex—the more advanced and evolutionarily recent part of the brain—that everything is fine may carry far less weight than the urgency of the fight-or-flight message. Think of a panic attack, in which intense bodily sensations of tension and a racing heart combine with feelings of fear or terror and thoughts about bad things that might happen. It's far from easy to simply sit with such "guests."

So it serves you to begin a practice of mindfulness medita-tion by relaxing your body and your mind as much as you can and creating conditions that'll help you be open to your expe-rience with calmness and equanimity. The practices that follow will help you relax, settle, and be open to what arises. You can practice them in sequence at the beginning of a period of meditation, or, if time is limited, you can practice one or more according to your preference. Most of the guided meditations are about fifteen minutes, and that's how long I normally recommend beginners meditate for. Once you have established a regular practice, you can set a timer and sit for fifteen, twenty, or thirty minutes or longer.

Practice 4: Calming and Welcoming

For each of these practices, find a quiet place and sit comfortably on a chair (or bench or cushion). Keeping your back straight, relax your shoulders and rest your hands in your lap (or on your knees or thighs), with your chest open so you can breathe easily. Allow your eyes to gently close. Or, if you prefer, leave them open, and let your gaze rest, soft and unfocused, a few feet in front of you.

Let your attention come into your body. Feel your breath in your nostrils and with the rising and falling of your chest and belly. Feel your body's contact with the surface beneath you.

Deep, Relaxed Breathing

Take a full, deep breath, filling your lungs. Pause for a few seconds before breathing out, then slowly breathe out until all your breath has been released. Breathe in deeply again, filling your body with breath, then slowly release; as you breathe out, imagine all of your stresses and cares are being released. As you breathe in deeply again, invite a quality of calm to your body and mind. You can silently say *Calm* as you breathe in and out, or say *Breathing in, calming the body; breathing out, calming the mind.* Take another couple of deep, relaxing breaths, in and out, and then let your breath settle into its own natural rhythm.

Progressive Relaxation of the Body

Bring your attention inward and scan your body, beginning at your scalp and moving down through your face to your torso and lower body. If you feel tension in any area as you do so, invite that area to relax.

Breathing in a relaxed way, pay particular attention to those areas where many of us tend to hold tension: the eyes, the face, the tongue, the jaw, the shoulders, the back of the neck, the upper back. Then drop down to the chest and belly, which we often clench when we're tense or under stress. Invite your belly to relax and soften, and let your breath come into a relaxed, open belly. Shift your attention down through your abdomen and groin to your legs, thighs, calves, and feet, and invite each area in turn to relax. Then slowly move your attention back up your body. If there's an area where you're still holding tension, pause there, and, breathing in a relaxed, easy way, invite a natural softening, letting go of any tension. Now bring awareness to your whole body and be at ease, receptive, and relaxed.

Inviting a Smile

Sitting in a relaxed and comfortable way, see how it feels to invite a smile to your face by activating the muscles at the corners of your mouth and your eyes. You don't need to be feeling particularly happy or joyful to relax and de-stress through smiling. Inviting a smile sends a message of safety and well-being to your brain and nervous system.

It can help to bring to mind someone who makes you feel happy, or a place where you feel peaceful and at ease. Allow yourself to sense any shifts in bodily feelings that come from your smile. Now, let your smile be the expression of how you wish to greet whatever arises for you. Smile into the tension in your shoulders; smile to greet an anxious thought; smile at the joys and the sorrows that come up. Welcome the "guests." And come back to the smile anytime in meditation—and in daily life.

"I am aware of..."

Many of us spend large swaths of our time lost in thought and disconnected from our bodies and emotions, from our aliveness. The Tibetan Buddhist teacher Chögyam Trungpa described our everyday human condition as "a huge traffic jam of discursive thought" (Trungpa 1999, 66). A simple and effective practice that can help you be more aware of your direct experience and live more fully in the present is to note what you're aware of from moment to moment.

This is a meditation that you can do almost anywhere—sitting comfortably and bringing awareness to whatever you notice, and naming or noting the sounds, sensations, emotions, thoughts, tastes, odors, and images that come into your consciousness. You can say, "I am aware of x" or simply note whatever is present—"tightness in belly," "sound of traffic."

Here's the transcript of a five-minute "aware of..." meditation I practiced on a plane coming back from London: *Aware of engine sound...tightness in chest and belly...deep breath...swallowing... tightness around my eyes...taking a deep breath...child's voice... someone coughs...tight throat...sound of a voice...rumble of engine...relaxing...hands on keyboard...coolness in air...feeling confined...cough...relaxed breath...darkness in cabin...lightness of screen...snippet of poem comes into my mind...thoughts about getting home...thought about seeing my mother...sadness around my eyes...swallowing...cool air in nostrils...voice...random letters typed from hands in confined space...sleepiness.*

And one I practiced in a coffee shop: *Aware of tightness in my belly...a song on the radio...pleasant feeling in response to the song...aware of voices...dryness in my mouth...taste of coffee... creaking of the door opening and closing...thought that "they should oil the door"...high voice of barista...someone asks if she can sit down...I nod and smile "yes"...pleasant song on radio... wondering who the singer is...creaking door...tightness in belly in response to creaking...song...pen pressing against fingers... creaking...looking at other customers...thinking how quickly the coffee shop has filled up.*

What's great about this practice is that nothing is "wrong" if you can simply be aware of it and note it. It helps you see that everything arises, stays for a time, and then passes. And if you can bring awareness to whatever is present without clinging or pushing away or judging, you can experience peace and well-being and alleviate stress and suffering.

Welcoming the "Guests"—
Summing Up

Mindfulness invites you to start where you are—to acknowledge that this moment, this experience, is "like this." There's a power and freedom that comes from being open to this moment just as it is. The image of your experiences, sensations, and thoughts—whether painful or pleasant, joyful or sorrowful—as "guests," who come to visit you for a time, can be helpful. If you can bring a welcoming attitude even to your more challenging experiences, they'll become less personal, less of a problem, and more like a weather system with patterns that may be intense but are also transient. You'll see that you can experience urges, strong emotions, challenging bodily sensations, and difficult thoughts without escaping into habitual and unhealthy behaviors.

Taking some time to calm your mind and body, cultivating a sense of ease and tranquility, can also help create the conditions to meet whatever experiences arise.

CHAPTER 5

Cultivating Attitudes of Mindfulness

If you are distressed by anything external, the pain is not
due to the thing itself, but to your estimate of it; and this
you have the power to revoke at any moment.

—Marcus Aurelius, *Meditations*

Focusing attention on your direct experience, which we'll
discuss more fully in the next chapter, is at the core of
mindfulness and is essential in transforming unhealthy
or unwanted habits. But attention isn't enough. You can be
very alert and attentive and wait for the exact moment to
make a biting or hurtful comment that might leave you feeling
remorseful or end a relationship. A pickpocket or burglar may
have exquisite focus and attention to commit his crimes successfully while being indifferent to the harm caused to his
victims and himself. A diligent meditator might be able to
develop deep states of concentration, but if she didn't

cultivate acceptance and self-compassion she could become disillusioned or doubt-ridden if painful or challenging emotions or mind states arose that she couldn't resolve simply by focusing her mind.

Your intentions are crucial, since they align your thoughts and actions with what you care about and aspire to most deeply. And your intentions and actions must be guided by an ethical understanding and approach to life—a commitment to living and acting in a wise, compassionate, and mindful way. Otherwise—if mindfulness was just about focused attention—you could continue to act out harmful habits, but in a more focused way. At the deepest level, you must ask yourself, *Does this thought or action lead to well-being, benefit, or happiness to myself and others, or does it lead to suffering and harm?* Then you can make choices that are likely to lead to well-being, peace, and harmony and avoid those choices that will likely lead to harm.

Also essential are the attitudes and qualities you bring to your experience. Key questions you can ask yourself at any time in meditation and daily life are: *How am I meeting this moment? What are the qualities of heart and mind with which I am responding to my experience here and now?*

In psychology, attitudes are seen as learned tendencies to evaluate certain things—for example, people, places, or situations—favorably or unfavorably. Therefore, attitudes can change. In Buddhist understanding and mindfulness practice, too, attitudes are seen as changeable. You can cultivate attitudes that support greater happiness and well-being and abandon those that lead to stress and suffering.

As you have learned, the core of a mindful approach to your experience is an attitude of receptivity to this moment as it unfolds. This receptivity is expressed variously as "welcoming your experience," "accepting," "allowing," "saying yes to what is," "not resisting (or judging or clinging)," "being open to," "being with your experience," and "letting be." All of these words, phrases, and images point to the same attitude or quality of mind—ending your conflict with this moment's experience, opening to this moment as it is. This constitutes not passivity, but rather a creative and dynamic engagement with your experience.

Some time ago I noticed something had shifted in the way I was driving. I was driving impatiently more often, seeing other motorists as "in my way," honking my horn more frequently, and arriving home more tense than usual. I wasn't aware of any particular reason for or event that explained this change. But since I was teaching a course on bringing mindfulness to unwanted habits, this pattern seemed like an area of my life that called for attention.

When I explored my intentions, it became clear that my main goal had been to get to my destination as quickly as possible. When I brought awareness to a deeper intention, I connected with a wish to be a kind and thoughtful driver, committed to arriving safely at my destination and wishing the same for other drivers.

Then when I examined my attitude, I saw that it was generally one of resisting what I was feeling in the moment and leaning into the future, which at the time seemed more important and pressing than the present. Being unaware of my attitude and my relationship to my experience, I was unconsciously acting out whatever urges or emotions were operating under the surface of my consciousness. And the more I continued not paying attention to my direct experience, the more habitual my pattern of impatient driving became, and the more it became my default mode.

Seeing the ways in which my intentions and attitudes weren't aligned with my deepest intentions or the attitudes I wished to bring to my experience and my life, I was able to establish a clear intention to drive thoughtfully and safely, with an attitude of kindness and acceptance. This allowed me to reset my "default" approach to driving. Now, when I find myself triggered by another driver's actions or by unexpected traffic, I come back to my intentions and return to the attitudes of friendliness and acceptance that embody those intentions.

Seven Attitudes of Mindfulness

Jon Kabat-Zinn, in his classic book on the practices of mindfulness-based stress reduction, *Full Catastrophe Living*, highlighted seven essential attitudes as the soil for cultivating mindful awareness (Kabat-Zinn 1990). These seven qualities provide a useful starting point for exploring the specific approaches to meeting this moment that are conducive to well-being and happiness:

Nonjudging is the quality of meeting your experience impartially, without evaluating it as good or bad, right or wrong, better or worse.

Patience is the attitude of allowing things to unfold and be experienced in their own time, without rushing them and losing your connection with the present moment.

Beginner's mind is the willingness to meet this moment with curiosity, as something fresh and never before experienced. As the Zen teacher Suzuki Roshi said, "In the beginner's mind there are many possibilities; in the expert's there are few" (Suzuki 1998, 21).

Trust is honoring your own authority, inner wisdom, and potential for growing and learning, as well as feeling confident that you can find a refuge in the present moment and meet life as it unfolds.

Nonstriving is cultivating an attitude of wise and balanced effort and seeing how you lose connection with the present moment and with yourself when you lean into the future to get somewhere or something.

Acceptance is being open to this moment and experiencing things just as they are without judgment, clinging, or resistance.

Letting go is cultivating an attitude of being open to your experience, seeing where you're clinging or attaching to an experience, and releasing your hold on it.

Kabat-Zinn's list of qualities is a helpful elaboration of important attitudes to develop consciously in mindfulness practice. Other qualities we might add include kindness, humor, ease, and determination. There's clearly no correct or complete list of qualities that support mindful presence, and there's significant overlap between these qualities, which complement and support each other. The key to their value lies in how effectively they help you wake up out of unconsciousness and find greater peace and freedom in your life.

What are the qualities of mind that best allow you to accept your experience—to be present, alive, and fully engaged?

Three Core Qualities That Support Mindfulness

In my own meditation and mindfulness practice as well as my work with others, I have found three qualities or attitudes of mind and heart to be essential:

- *Kindness*—toward yourself and your experience, as well as others

- *Curiosity* or interest in what you're experiencing

- *Acceptance* of what's unfolding—the good, the bad, and the ugly

Let's look at each of these qualities, how they support mindful presence, and how they can help you work with unhealthy habits.

Kindness

Because many of us are prone to self-judgment and self-criticism, you may need to nurture and develop kindness toward yourself and your experience.

I met recently with a student who remarked on how difficult it was to be kind to herself. Whenever she tried to be kind to herself, she said, "What comes up right away in my mind is, 'Who am I to deserve that? I haven't earned it.'" If you, similarly, tend to judge yourself harshly or feel a lack of self-worth, the practice of meeting with kindness whatever arises can help you be open to and see the impermanence of these harsh voices of self-criticism. In later chapters, we'll look at skills to help you investigate these deeply rooted beliefs (chapter 7) and meet your experience with self-compassion (chapter 9) to give you some additional support in working with self-judgment and harsh self-criticism.

Kindness directly counters negative patterns of thought. So, if while you're meditating a self-judging thought comes up—*I'm so lazy*, or *unfocused*, or *judgmental*—you can name that as "judging" and meet it with as much kindness and self-compassion as possible, perhaps putting your hand on your heart and saying "forgiven" or "peace."

If you can continually meet your habits of self-judgment and criticism in a field of kindness that doesn't make the thoughts and judgments wrong, but recognizes them as conditioned and impersonal movements of your mind, their hard edges will begin to soften and dissolve.

As you bring kindness to your own experience, space will open in your heart, allowing you to meet the suffering of others with compassion as well. Naomi Shihab Nye expresses this in her poem "Kindness":

...Before you learn the tender gravity of kindness,
You must travel where the Indian in a white poncho
lies dead by the side of the road.
You must see how this could be you,
how he too was someone
who journeyed through the night with plans
and the simple breath that kept him alive...

(Shihab Nye 1995, 42)

Unless you practice kindness toward yourself, mindfulness can reinforce the sense that you're a flawed person, and you'll keep trying to get rid of or change the "bad" parts of yourself. Changing your habit will become a self-improvement project. With kindness, mindful awareness will help you be open to the fullness of your humanity and see your experiences less personally. It'll allow you the space to forgive yourself when you lapse into old habits or fall short of your objectives and to begin again—to come back to your intention to change your habits—without the baggage of guilt and self-recrimination.

Curiosity

Curiosity is the quality of being interested in what's occurring. It arises naturally out of paying attention to your experience in a nonjudging way, and it's a quality that you can consciously cultivate as well.

Curiosity is an antidote to boredom. When you're bored, it means you have lost contact with your direct experience and have bought into a story in your mind, such as *This isn't interesting; I wish I was doing something else.* Instead of believing the story your mind tells you that this moment should be different, you can investigate the feelings that are present. Let the thought that whatever is happening is boring go, and see what happens when you pay close attention to your emotions and bodily sensations.

As psychologist Fritz Perls said, "Boredom is lack of attention" (cited in Goldstein 1993, 80). Meditators sometimes feel bored when focusing on their breath in meditation, but when they focus on their breath more closely—experiencing the subtly different sensations in their nostrils or torso, or the feeling of release that can come with a deep exhalation— their breath can become much more interesting. In the same way, anything that seems humdrum or banal can reveal hidden depths when you shine the spotlight of your attention on it. The writer Henry Miller described this shift in attitude:

"The moment one gives close attention to anything, even a blade of grass, it becomes a mysterious, awesome, indescribably magnificent world in itself" (cited in Chang 2006, 67). Mindfulness and investigation are the first two of seven qualities that the Buddha taught as "factors of awakening"—qualities that lead to freedom or enlightenment. (The other five are energy, joy, tranquility, concentration, and equanimity.)

Try bringing curiosity to your experience now, by bringing your awareness fully to three breaths and noticing with interest whatever sensations and feelings come up—coolness, tightness, relief, expansion, whatever is present.

Another simple practice is to open your hand and gaze at your palm for one minute. What do you notice when you pay close attention: lines, colors, texture, contours, folds, veins, wrinkles? Is it more interesting than the *thought* or *concept* of looking at your palm?

The next time you're experiencing a difficult emotion, try turning that same curiosity toward the way you feel. Rather than getting swept up in the emotion, examine the strong energies that are present. How do they manifest in your body—as tightness, tension, heat, or flushing? Do they flow and ebb slowly, like the tide, or do they land with successive crashes, like waves? Do they become stronger or weaker, or do they stay pretty much the same? Do they move around, metamorphosing from one feeling into another?

Becoming familiar with uncomfortable or unpleasant feelings is a key skill in overcoming unhealthy habits. Bringing awareness to your experience changes your relationship to it. For example, after Roy, whom you met in chapter 1, tried bringing curiosity to his habit of eating sweets, he reported: "The initial intense focus the first few evenings on [my] late-night sugar and carb bingeing was incredibly fruitful. There's a lesson there for me, one that I have learned before and will probably need to learn again: when desiring to break an addiction or change a habit, study it with some intensity at first, bring your concentration to bear, be fearless, have the detachment of a naturalist studying an animal, and stick with it long enough to get some insight. Seems so obvious now… but in the beginning it feels like quite a revelation and very hard to do."

Acceptance

Acceptance of your experience is at the core of mindful awareness. You can't be mindful if you don't accept your experience, if you're in conflict with it. And for acceptance to be freeing, it must be genuine and wholehearted rather than conditional or partial. Meditation teacher Tara Brach termed this *radical* acceptance (Brach 2003). If your attitude is *I'll accept this pain as long as it goes away in the next five minutes*, it's one of bargaining rather than acceptance. When you bargain, your focus is on a future outcome—in this case, the end of the pain—rather than your experience as it is. The focus on when the pain will end takes you away from the present moment. So, if you become aware that your acceptance is partial or conditional, be open to the resistance, meet it with kindness, and establish the intention to meet whatever sensations, emotions, or thoughts arise with full acceptance.

To give you an example of acceptance, let's say you're meditating and you have the thought *Something terrible is going to happen*. You don't have to believe this thought, but you don't have to try to get rid of it either. You can accept that this thought exists and meet it with kindness and interest. You can analyze it, asking yourself *Is this thought really true?* Or *Is this thought helpful to me right now?* Or you can simply observe the thought and let it go, returning to awareness of your breath or your body.

In the mid-1990s I participated in a silent meditation retreat at a Thai temple in India, a short walk from the site of the Buddha's awakening. I practiced sitting and walking meditation for five or six days, and my prevailing feeling during that time was that I had to "get somewhere." There was something I needed to see and know that I wasn't seeing and knowing—and once I "got" what I was missing I would experience a deep freedom.

Somewhere around the sixth day I let go of the searching—or, more accurately, the intense searching fell away. What remained was an experience of deep peace and serenity. I hadn't "gotten" anywhere, but ending the struggle to be somewhere that I was not brought inner peace and happiness. Tibetan Buddhist teacher Chögyam Trungpa put it this way: "There is no need to struggle to be free; the ending of the struggle is itself freedom" (Trungpa 1999, 46–47).

When you bring these three attitudes of awareness to your experience—kindness, curiosity, and acceptance—you'll create the conditions for transforming established patterns of thought and behavior.

Bringing Attitudes of Mindfulness to Unwanted Habits

As discussed briefly in chapter 2, different kinds of habits have different feelings associated with them, but all can be changed when met with a kind, interested, and accepting awareness. I highlighted four main categories of habits— habits of *wanting*, habits of *distraction*, habits of *resistance*, and habits of *doing*—that incorporate many of the most common behaviors that people seek to change.

Habits of Wanting

Habits of wanting, craving, or addiction have an energy and "feeling tone" of moving toward something that you desire. Your body and mind focus in on the object—be it a drink, drugs, food, cigarettes, sex, or any other object of desire—and your sense of well-being and happiness becomes tied to getting what you crave. Working mindfully with habits of wanting means being fully open to the feeling of wanting as it manifests—in your body, your emotions, and your mind. If something triggers the urge, you can be open to the sensations, feelings, and emotions, say yes to them, and meet them with kindness, interest, and acceptance. If a thought arises such as *I'll feel better if I have a smoke/drink*, meet that thought with kindness. Choose to acknowledge what's happening in your body and your emotions without acting on it. When you learn to recognize and allow the uncomfortable, unpleasant, or difficult feelings, you'll weaken the hold that the craving has over you. You'll become less identified with the habit—"I'm a drinker" or "smoker" or "compulsive eater"—and the urges and habits will become less "me" or "mine."

Habits of Distraction

With habits of distraction—such as checking your phone every other minute or spending large amounts of time on social media or watching TV—the initial challenge may be to know that your attention has wandered and you have lost contact with your intentions and plans.

When you become aware that your attention has moved into an unwanted or unhealthy habit—or if you can catch yourself before moving into it—bring a close attention to your bodily experience and emotions. Is there an uncomfortable bodily feeling that you want to escape from—perhaps some tension or agitation in the body? Stay with these sensations and feelings, then bring to mind the question: *What must I experience if I don't turn toward my habitual behavior?* Perhaps the answer is a feeling of tightness, numbness, or restlessness. Meet the experience with a kind, curious, and accepting attention. See how, when met in this way, the feeling will come and go in its own time.

You can meet emotions such as fear, anxiety, and anger with the same receptive attitude. And when thoughts of moving away from what feels unpleasant toward immediate gratification arise, reflect on what matters most to you. Will you be happier with a feeling of temporary relief that reinforces the unhealthy habit? Or do you wish to move toward greater well-being, health, and peace? Then, choose to stay with what's present without acting mindlessly or out of habit.

Habits of Resisting

Habits of resisting, which manifest as frustration, annoyance, impatience, anger, judgment, and similar emotions and mind states, tend to have a different "feeling tone." You feel as if you're defending yourself, resisting a threat, or protecting yourself from something that will harm you. Often you'll feel tightness, tension, contraction, agitation, heat, or other "fight-or-flight" sensations. The accompanying thoughts or beliefs may urge you to act in a way that will change this unpleasant situation or experience. Think about feeling impatient in a store when someone seems to be taking "too long" to finish a purchase, or being stuck in traffic when you're running late. You'll typically feel a tightness in certain muscles—often the chest or belly or face—linked to thoughts like *This person/situation/experience shouldn't be like this, I need to do something to change this,* or *I need to solve this problem.*

You can meet habits of resistance in the same way that you respond to habits of wanting and distraction: by bringing your attention back to what you're experiencing right now, then meeting what's here with a kind, curious, and accepting awareness. Bringing awareness to your breath will help ease feelings of tightness and tension. Putting your hand on your heart can help bring you back into awareness of your body and temper thoughts of needing to do something. Sending a wish of peace and well-being to yourself, perhaps whispering "May I be peaceful," can create a sense of inner space to hold the difficult experience and sensations. Here, too, the practice is to bring a kind, curious, and accepting attitude to what's present—choosing to stay with your direct experience rather than moving into habitual behavior. The Tibetan Buddhist teacher Yongey Mingyur Rinpoche stated the choice clearly: "Ultimately, happiness comes down to choosing between the discomfort of becoming aware of your mental afflictions and the discomfort of being ruled by them" (Yongey Mingyur 2007, 250).

Habits of Doing

Habits of doing typically involve feeling as though you're always on your way somewhere, as though something bad will happen if you don't keep moving and getting things done. You may think, *Things will be okay if I can just accomplish the next task.* You may feel frenetic, agitated, intense, or stressed out.

You can respond to these habits with the same attitude of kind, interested, and accepting awareness. Begin by coming back to what you're feeling now—physically, emotionally, and mentally. Invite yourself to experience all the sensations and emotions associated with that frantic energy without identifying with that energy. Mindfulness practice will help prevent you from getting swept up in the story of "I need to get this done or things will fall apart."

These four kinds of habits aren't mutually exclusive. A craving for something that you think will make you feel good, such as eating something sweet, is often accompanied by a desire to avoid an unpleasant feeling—for example, tension, worry, tightness, or numbness. Similarly, when you disconnect from the present moment by spending large amounts of time online, there's often a feeling of discomfort, anxiety, or tension that you're subconsciously seeking to escape. With each of these habitual patterns, the remedy is the same: return to your present-moment experience and meet it with interest, friendliness, and acceptance.

Practice 5: Meditation on Attitude

This is a meditation that involves being aware of the attitudes you're bringing to your experience. It involves asking, *Am I meeting this moment in a welcoming way? Or with resistance or judgment?* It's a practice you can incorporate into formal meditation periods, as well as at different times in your daily life.

Sit comfortably, and allow yourself to relax and settle. Close your eyes, and let your attention rest in your body. Take a few full breaths, on each out-breath releasing any tension you might be holding. Invite your body to relax, slowly moving your attention down and up your body, inviting a softening of any area where you're holding tension.

For fifteen minutes or until the end of your meditation period, be open to whatever you're experiencing in an accepting and nonjudging way. If it helps ground you, maintain a relaxed awareness of your breathing.

To help bring awareness to your moment-to-moment experience and cultivate kindness, interest, and acceptance, attitudes that support well-being and happiness, periodically bring awareness to your experience and notice your attitude at that moment. Is there a feeling of being on your way somewhere? Are you tensing or defending yourself against something? Are you resisting your experience? Does your relationship to this moment feel friendly and kind? Is there a quality of welcoming or allowing what's present to be here? Or an attitude of pushing away? If your attitude is one of resistance, clinging, or judging, consciously evoke an attitude of kindness to yourself and your experience. You can put your hand on your heart and wish yourself well: "May I be at peace…may I be happy." Invite an attitude of interest to your experience. *What am I aware of? How does it feel?* Consciously say yes to whatever you're experiencing by accepting, welcoming, and allowing what's present to be just as it is. Bring a half smile to your face, relax the muscles at the corners of your mouth and eyes, and offer the welcoming attitude of a smile to whatever arises.

Cultivating Attitudes of Mindfulness—Summing Up

Mindfulness involves paying attention, but paying attention in a particular way. *How* you meet your experience is a key element of mindfulness. So are three qualities or attitudes you bring to your practice: kindness, curiosity, and acceptance. Together they'll help you be present for your experience and counter your tendencies to move habitually toward what you like and resist what you don't like.

Kindness will counter negative or judging patterns of thought and open space for you to be able to experience challenging sensations, emotions, and mind states. When you bring *curiosity* to your experience, you'll no longer be swept up in or so identified with your experience. Being curious will allow you to step out of your mind's story or narrative and into your direct experience. And *acceptance* will invite you to meet your experience wholeheartedly and without resistance. When you accept your experience fully, you'll no longer be caught up in it or defined by it.

You can bring these attitudes to different kinds of habits, including habits of *wanting, resisting, distraction,* and *doing.* Any time you bring awareness to your experience, you change your relationship to it. When you meet habitual behaviors with friendliness, interest, and acceptance, their hold over you will tend to weaken, enabling you to abandon unwanted or unhealthy habits and cultivate more beneficial ones.

CHAPTER 6

Harnessing the Power of Attention

The faculty of voluntarily bringing back a wandering attention over and over again is the very root of judgment, character and will... An education which should improve this faculty would be the education par excellence.

—William James, *The Principles of Psychology*

Over the years, many of my students have shared that mindfulness has helped them change long-standing habits, and more than a few have reported that it saved their life.

Steve's Story

At a weekend silent meditation retreat I was teaching, one day Steve, the retreat manager, asked whether he could have a word with me after breakfast. "I know I shouldn't talk, but I want to share with you what I realized today: it's okay to be still!" Steve said he felt a deep sense of relief and well-being in knowing that there was nothing to fear in stillness.

I first met Steve in late 2006. He had contacted me for individual mindfulness counseling after attending a daylong meditation workshop I had taught. Steve had recently retired after twenty-seven years as an army officer, having served in Iraq and many other zones of conflict. He had been in the Pentagon in the part of the E-Ring—the outer area of the building, occupied by senior officials—that was struck directly by a hijacked plane on September 11, 2001. Two minutes before the plane hit, he had been with the general, who died when the plane crashed into his office. When the plane hit, Steve was knocked down by debris, lost consciousness, came to, and was helped out of the building through the smoke, ash, and water. For some years afterward, he had no wish to attend memorials or other events related to the attack or even discuss his experience.

But the patterns that created stress and trauma in Steve's life began long before the events of September 11. His working-class, ethnic upbringing in New York taught him how to be tough. He learned that it was not manly, and could be dangerous, to show his feelings. The way you survived and made it in the world was to "suck it up." Joining the army was a natural choice.

Steve did well at West Point and was promoted to captain, major, then colonel ahead of his classmates. The army taught him how to suppress his fear and respond automatically under threat. What the military never taught him was to feel or express emotion.

For two decades, Steve's army career flourished. He was trusted by his superiors, and he was liked and respected by those under his command. But his marriage fell apart, and his relationship with his kids grew distant. The pressure to "stuff" his feelings intensified. In the first Iraq war (Operation Desert Storm), Steve drove down the Highway of Death from Kuwait into Iraq and witnessed the carnage. "The only way I could deal with this horror was to believe it was a good thing, that it had to happen, and that our enemies were less than human," he said.

As the pressure built, particularly after 9/11, Steve took refuge in alcohol and the prescription drugs that gave him temporary relief. He was able to leave the army honorably, but addicted. For a year and a half, he isolated himself before seeking help by checking into a recovery program.

In the years we worked together, Steve practiced opening himself to the feelings that he had suppressed for decades. He learned that even the most difficult emotions lasted for only a time and that it was possible to ride even intense waves of sensation and emotion. "I learned that I could let myself feel what I'm feeling. Sometimes it felt like my whole body was going to explode, but I learned that I could stay. I really believe this practice has rewired my brain. I can feel pain and be with it in a different way."

Steve shared that what most inspired him about mindfulness was learning that change is possible. "When I began this practice, I couldn't get on an elevator or sit in a room without being anxious and fidgety and wanting to run out. Now I know that even when old habits and patterns return, I have the tools to stay with the feelings and see that they pass. I know peace and stillness are possible even in difficult times."

As of this writing, Steve has rebuilt a warm and loving relationship with his kids. He recently graduated from a two-year meditation teacher–training program I co-taught, and he's working on a PhD in psychology. "At times I forget and get pulled back toward old habits," he says, "but I always know I can come back to awareness, to the inner stillness I have touched, and can begin again."

Paying attention to your direct experience is at the core of mindfulness. In Buddhist teachings, suffering arises from not seeing things as they really are. Freedom from suffering comes from taking refuge in reality, in the truth of how things are, by being open to your experience as it is. In the words of the Buddha: "In the seen there will be just be the seen, in the heard just the heard, in the sensed, just the sensed, in the imagined just the imagined" (Kornfield 1996, 67).

To illustrate, imagine a friend walks by without greeting you. If you have a habit of judging yourself harshly and believe that others have a low opinion of you, you might interpret your friend's lack of acknowledgment as a deliberate slight. You might fall into a spiral of negative thoughts and judgments about your friend's unkindness or your own unworthiness. But if you can meet those thoughts and judgments with kindness, you'll see them as nothing more than passing phenomena. If you can be open to any unpleasant bodily sensations or emotions that you're experiencing as a result of the perceived snub, you can offer yourself compassion and wish yourself well. You can reflect kindly about your friend and consider the possibility that she didn't see you or was preoccupied. And if your friend might have been sending a message by her silence, you can commit to having a conversation with her about any difficulties or misunderstandings in your relationship.

As you train yourself to pay attention by focusing on a particular object such as your breath or sounds in your environment, you'll strengthen your faculty of mindfulness. With practice, you'll be more able to bring this kind, nonjudging attention to your habitual behaviors, such as eating compulsively or checking social media whenever you're bored.

Paying Attention Before, During, and After

You can work on undoing an unhealthy habit by exercising present-moment awareness at three distinct times: *before* the impulse to engage in the habit arises, *during* the impulse to engage in the habit, and *after* the impulse to engage in the habit has subsided (or been indulged).

- *Before*: You can explore what leads you to engage in the habit and make choices that can help prevent you from doing so.

- *During*: You can pay attention and choose to be open to the urge, craving, or difficult feeling that typically spurs the habitual behavior, gently focusing on that feeling and allowing it to come and go rather than engaging in the habit.

- *After*: If you engaged in the habit, you can consciously extend yourself kindness and forgiveness, rather than compounding an unhealthy habit with negative judgments or harsh self-criticism.

Practice 6: Awareness of Habits— Before, During, and After

Here are some examples of ways you can work at changing a habit at these three different points.

Before: Bring awareness to the habit that you want to change, and think about the situations or conditions that trigger the habit. Are there actions you can take to avoid acting out of habit? What might be an alternative, healthier choice? For example:

- If at home you frequently snack on sweets when you're feeling anxious, uncertain, confused, or lonely, ensure that you don't have sweets in the house. Purchase healthier foods, such as nuts or fruit, to have on hand when you wish to snack.

- If you typically drink more alcohol than is good for you when you get together with a particular friend, propose meeting for a hike or coffee rather than for happy hour.

- If you have a habit of procrastinating when you think about working on an important project, make a commitment to yourself to work on it for a limited time each day—say fifteen to thirty minutes, twice a day.

- If you often find yourself driving impatiently or aggressively because you need to be at work or at an appointment on time, plan (if possible) to add a ten- or fifteen-minute cushion to your travel time, and commit to driving in a conscious and relaxed way as you begin your journey.

Once you bring awareness to the habit urge and notice how and when it typically arises, you can take steps to keep it from arising. And you can be prepared with alternative, more positive responses if it does arise.

During: Pay attention to the context or environment in which the habit urge typically arises—the place, time, people, sights, sounds, and smells. For example, perhaps you find the smell of sweet, sticky buns in a mall or airport irresistible and find yourself buying and eating them without consciously deciding to do so. If so, whenever you're in a mall or airport, pay close attention to what you're experiencing. Then, when you first become aware of the craving for a bun, take a few deep breaths and bring awareness to your internal experience. Perhaps your stomach is tight or your mouth is watering. Make a conscious choice to remain aware of your direct experience, rather than acting on the craving.

Pay close attention to your bodily sensations, and notice how none of the sensations or feelings stays very long. Be aware of how the sensations ebb and flow, perhaps becoming more intense, or lessening, or fading for a while, then reappearing. Name the sensations, if this is helpful: *tightness, shortness of breath, pressure, heat, racing heart.* You can visualize the sensations as waves that rise and fall.

If you become aware of a strong emotion, such as anxiety, that you have responded to with comfort food in the past, name it and be open to your bodily sensations and emotions, bringing awareness to the thoughts and urges that may accompany them. Then, with kindness, let those thoughts and urges go. Recall and connect with your deepest intention—for example, to live a conscious and healthy life—and reflect on how staying with your direct experience and meeting it with kindness and care aligns with your intentions and values. If you feel like eating something, choose something healthful. And, if you can, prepare in advance to make an alternative and healthier choice the next time you feel the craving.

After: If you successfully resisted the impulse to engage in the habit, let yourself feel whatever comes up. Perhaps it's a feeling of relief or release, or gratitude that you were able to respond mindfully, or a feeling of optimism that change is possible. Take these feelings in. Appreciate any positive bodily sensations, emotions, or thoughts. Take in the good feelings. If negative or neutral feelings arise, meet them too with kindness and care.

If you failed to resist the impulse to engage in the habit, meet whatever feelings come up with kindness. If self-judgment or harsh criticism arises, hold these feelings and thoughts with care and compassion. Similarly, if frustration or pessimism arises, meet it with friendliness. You can put your hand on your heart and say, "I care about this suffering" or "forgiven."

As a way of learning from this experience, think back to the conditions that led you to act on the urge and explore whether there was a point at which you might have made a different choice. Did you suffer a lapse in awareness? Did a change in the situation or the arrival of a strong emotion lead you to act on the impulse to engage in the habit? Did the craving feel too strong to resist?

What might have helped you make a choice that was more in alignment with your deepest values and intentions? Revisit what matters most to you and how working to abandon this unhealthy or unwanted habit supports your deepest intentions. Remember, you can begin again in any moment, and choose to begin again.

Roy (who you may recall from chapter 1 has a sugar craving) practiced bringing awareness to his experience before, during, and after his cravings.

Roy's Story—Continued

Knowing the temptation of walking past the mini-mart that sold packs of delicious chewy cookies, Roy sometimes took a different way home. "Some nights, I'm choosing to stop at the supermarket and buy carrots and hummus as an alternative," he said. "Some nights I still binge."

Also helpful for Roy was to see his craving in the larger context of his life. "I have never before thought so regularly about things like *Is my weekly schedule balanced? Does it have the right kinds of things in it? Is the mix right? Whom am I seeing too much of? Whom too little?* And on a daily basis I try to meditate for forty-five minutes, get some exercise that makes me sweat, do some yoga, do something outside of work with someone or a group of people who are good for me to hang out with, read and listen to something good, and look for ways I can be focused on others and possibly help someone out. I don't worry much if I can't tick all those boxes. If I'm getting most of them most of the time and not starving any one of them in particular, I'm all right."

As noted earlier, Roy chose to focus closely on the direct experience of craving when he felt compelled to binge on sweets late in the evening. One of the strategies that he found most helpful was to substitute something healthy (or at times, less unhealthful) for the sweets. "I'm letting go of ice cream more of the time—sometimes substituting nothing, sometimes meditation or yoga, sometimes something less damaging than an entire pint of high-fat ice cream yet still pretty awful, like a bag of chocolate candies. With cigarettes and alcohol I could just put them down and work on substituting something else into my life. With sweet bingeing, if I can't substitute something else in a complete way, I look for something less harmful, then just enjoy it while trying to keep self-kindness in mind."

Whenever Roy did succumb to a craving, he met his lapse with kindness: "I am now able to more readily and frequently ride the wave of self-flagellation with a bit of detachment and find some kindness and friendliness toward myself."

Roy recognized that bringing greater awareness to his craving for sweets, and living more consciously and healthfully, is a journey rather than a destination. Supportive friends, increased consciousness of his schedule and diet, and a daily practice of meditation and yoga were all aids to greater awareness. "I've lost five pounds and gained a notch in my belt. Yet some nights are still a struggle—but I'm meeting them with more lightness, humor, and equanimity."

The Two Forms of Self-Awareness

In the past decade, neuroscientists have discovered that mindfulness training changes the structure and functioning of the brain. Among the most interesting and relevant to the understanding of the role of mindfulness in habit change is a 2007 study by Norman Farb and colleagues.

Using functional magnetic resonance imaging (fMRI), Farb and colleagues studied the brain activity of a group of participants who were new to mindfulness and compared it to the brain activity of a group of participants who had attended an eight-week mindfulness course. The researchers found two distinct forms of self-awareness: a *narrative focus*—which they called the default mode network—that was associated with rumination, self-referencing, mind-wandering, and more negative feelings; and an *experiencing focus*: seeing moment-to-moment experiences as transient events, which was associated with more positive feelings. Those participants who had been trained in mindfulness were better able to access the experiencing mode and uncouple from the narrative mode (Farb et al. 2007).

This and other studies (for example, Mason et al. 2007) point to two different ways of being aware of your experience. In a resting state, if you're not paying attention to your direct experience, you typically default to narrative mode. In narrative mode, you're comparing yourself with others, thinking about the past or future, and generally ruminating. But if you can bring awareness to what's present, you'll be less subject to mind-wandering and rumination, and experiencing mode will become your default mode.

Farb and colleagues suggest that the present-centered, experiencing mode may have been the original mode of self-awareness of our ancestors and that the narrative mode of self-reference may represent "an over-learned mode of information processing that has become automatic through practice" (Farb et al. 2007, 319). One way to characterize the narrative mode of self-awareness, then, is as a downside of modern humans' ability to process information and imagine future possibilities.

Studies on the default mode network of the brain are important in understanding the role of mindfulness in transforming unwanted habits. They point to the ways in which mindfulness training can help you overcome the habits of rumination and mind-wandering, which can spur unhealthy behaviors and thought patterns. Training in paying attention to the present moment can free you from the suffering that comes from being lost in discursive thought, opening you to the freedom that's here in each moment.

The Art of Paying Attention

In meditation, there are many different objects of attention, or "anchors," that you can use to sharpen your focus and deepen your concentration. For example, you can use:

- A mantra—a word or phrase that you focus on and return to

- An external object—such as a candle, sounds, or images

- A bodily sensation

- A visualization or mental image

- A koan (a paradoxical question in Zen Buddhism), such as "What's the sound of one hand clapping?"

- A philosophical question, such as "Who am I?"

In mindfulness meditation, your object of attention is typically an aspect of your direct experience—your breath, your bodily sensations, sounds in your environment, or (in walking meditation) the movement of your body.

If you're like most people, given the tendency for the mind to wander and get caught up in the content of your thoughts and emotions, it's important to train your mind in *focused attention* by concentrating on one thing, such as your breath. In this way, you'll learn to deepen your capacity to stay focused and to return to your object of meditation when your attention gets pulled away.

One of the most common objects of attention in mindfulness and other forms of meditation is your breath. Your breath can be an excellent object of attention, for several reasons:

- It's readily available—as long as you're alive, you're breathing.

- It's a relatively neutral object. People don't tend to feel overly positive or negative about their breath.

- It's a good barometer of your overall level of stress or relaxation. Your breath tends to be short and tight when you're under stress and fuller and deeper when you're relaxed.

- Focusing on your breath often has a calming effect.

Practicing mindfulness of breathing is relatively straightforward: You bring conscious awareness to the experience of breathing. The Buddha's instructions on mindfulness of breathing begin, "mindful he breathes in, mindful he breathes out…. Breathing in long, he knows, 'I breathe in long'… breathing in short, he knows, 'I breathe in short'" (Anālayo 2003, 126). The challenge is to sustain your attention on your breath rather than on anything that might feel more compelling—a memory of a discussion you had recently, your to-do list for the day ahead, images from a movie you saw recently, or fantasies about a new relationship or an exciting job. So, the practice of mindfulness of breathing involves:

- *Focusing* your attention on the object of awareness—your breath

- *Sustaining* your attention on your breath in the face of other experiences (whether internal or external) that compete for your attention

- *Monitoring* where your attention is and noticing when it has drifted

- *Withdrawing* your attention from thoughts when you become aware of being caught up in thinking

- *Redirecting* your attention to your breath without judgment

This last item is key. When practicing mindfulness of breathing, it's important that you meet any "lapse" of attention with kindness and nonjudgment, acknowledging that creating distracting thoughts is simply what the mind does. Think of your mind as a restless puppy. A puppy loves to scamper around, but you can train it (with kindness and diligence) to sit and respond to directions.

As with training a puppy, neither harshness nor laxness is effective in training your mind. Rather than seeing your wandering mind as a problem, try to celebrate the fact that you can wake up out of your plans, memories, or daydreams and experience this moment of wakefulness. And then come back to your breath—in-breath, out-breath—again and again.

Learning to stay with your breath or another object of meditation will strengthen your capacity to be open to difficult experiences, including strong impulses, cravings, and challenging emotions. Unless you practice opening yourself to strong emotions, powerful moods, or uncomfortable bodily sensations, they'll sweep you into habitual patterns again and again.

To sustain your focus on your breath, it can be helpful to open yourself to the feeling of your breath in your body and see where the sensations of breathing feel most relaxing to you. It might be your nostrils, where the coolness of the air coming in gives you a sense of well-being, or your chest or belly, where breathing out gives you a sense of ease. Make this your "home base" to which you can return whenever you become aware your attention has drifted.

If your mind is active and it's hard to focus on your breath, try counting breaths. One method is to count by one for each out-breath until you reach ten, then begin again at one—and any time your mind drifts into thought, or you lose count, just return again to one.

How Can the Art of Paying Attention Help You Change Unhelpful Habits?

Once you learn to pay attention more closely to your experience through mindfulness practice, you'll begin to see the ways in which cues and triggers in your environment or in your mind and body lead you to engage in habitual patterns of behavior. For example, perhaps it's loneliness that often leads you to reach unconsciously for a cigarette. With awareness, rather than smoke a cigarette, you can simply observe that feeling of loneliness until it passes. If you can be open to the experiences, such as feelings of loneliness, that typically trigger your habit urge, you can make choices that are more in alignment with your values and goals.

A friend and colleague of mine emphasized how much the benefits of mindfulness depend on practice: "If there's one thing I'm hit over the head with repeatedly it's that [mindfulness] is a practice—a long-term commitment that takes time and repetition for changes to occur. I might not realize that changes are happening until much after the fact, but boy, are they happening. In the process, things sometimes feel worse before they feel better because I'm so much more aware that I'm feeling anything at all. Things that I had pushed away— habits of eating and drinking to relieve stress that I wasn't paying attention to—I'm now more willing to look in the face. And that's difficult at times. But I know the way out, as someone said, is through."

In a recent study (Moore and Malinowski 2009), researchers compared a group of mindfulness meditators with a group of non-meditators using a well-known test of attention—the Stroop test. In the Stroop test, subjects are shown color words (for example, "red") that are sometimes actually a different color (for example, blue). When asked to identify the color of each word, most subjects take longer to respond when the color doesn't match the word. This is because their brains automatically process the *meaning* of the word, which interferes with their ability to say what it is they actually *see* (the color of the word).

The study found that meditators performed better than non-meditators on all measures of attention, as well as demonstrated greater cognitive flexibility—the "human ability to adapt cognitive processing strategies to face new and unexpected conditions." This suggested that, through training in mindfulness, cognitive processes that had become automatized could "be brought back under cognitive control and that previously automatic responses could be interrupted or inhibited" (Moore and Malinowski 2009, 182–83). In other words, with mindfulness, even decades-old habits can be brought into awareness and changed.

Practice 7: Mindfulness of Breathing Meditation

Take a few moments to relax your body and mind, letting your awareness come into your body. Take some full, deep breaths; on each out-breath, relax and let go of the stresses and cares of your day.

Invite a half-smile to the corners of your mouth and eyes, and visualize meeting everything you experience with the welcoming expression of a smile.

Sit in a way that's both relaxed and alert. With your eyes closed, if this is comfortable for you, or with your eyes open and your gaze soft and unfocused, bring your attention to the sensations of breathing—the feeling of breathing in and breathing out. As you breathe in, know that you're breathing in, and as you breathe out, know you're breathing out. Allow your breath to be just as it is, without trying to deepen it or change it in any way.

If it's helpful, mentally note *In* as you breathe in and *Out* as you breathe out. Or silently say *Rise* and *Fall* as your chest and belly rise and fall.

Establish a "home base" wherever your breath is most noticeable or feels most relaxing. It might be at your chest or belly, or at your nostrils where the cool air enters and the warm air is released. Let your attention rest in the direct experience of your body breathing.

Any time you become aware that your attention is no longer on your breath, if self-judgment or annoyance comes up, meet it with kindness. If it's helpful, silently label whatever mental activity it was that drew your attention—if you were planning your day, remembering a conversation, or daydreaming, note *planning*, *remembering*, or *daydreaming*—and gently bring your attention back to your in-breath and out-breath without judging or criticizing yourself. Do this for fifteen minutes or until the end of your meditation period.

In meditation, once your attention is stabilized on your breath or another object of meditation, you can be open to all aspects of your experience as they arise and pass—everything that enters your awareness through your five senses, as well as thoughts, emotions, moods, urges, and mind states. The following meditation will help you practice expanding your awareness.

Practice 8: Body Awareness Meditation

Pause whatever you have been doing and come into stillness, sitting comfortably. Let your eyes gently close, or keep them half open with a soft gaze a few feet ahead of you. Bring awareness to your body and whatever sensations are present.

Feel your body's contact with the surface beneath you, being open to whatever sensations are present—hardness, pressure, heat, tingling, pulsing, and so on. Feel the contact of your feet with the floor and the contact of any part of your body with another part—for example, your hands in your lap or on your knees. Feel the sensations in your chest and belly, breathing with whatever is present.

Bring awareness to your breathing, and notice whether your breathing is relaxed or tense. Meet your breathing as it is, and invite your breathing and your body to relax.

As you bring awareness to your body, let yourself feel whatever sensations are present. Watch them come and go; watch them ebb and flow. If the sensations cause you any stress or tension or anxiety, meet it with a kind and friendly attitude. Do this for fifteen minutes or until the end of your meditation period.

Eating is an area in which unhealthy habits are strong for many people. Perhaps you have a habit of eating in response to emotions or strong cravings rather than consciously and from need, or perhaps you have a habit of eating without awareness, scarcely aware of the taste of the food. A formal eating meditation practice can help you bring greater awareness to the experience of eating by slowing the process down and paying close attention to the details—touch, aroma, taste, sensations, thoughts, urges—of eating.

Practice 9: Eating Meditation

Begin by taking a simple piece of food, such as a raisin or grape, in your hand. Hold it in the palm of your hand or between your forefinger and thumb.

Imagine you have never seen this type of food before. Focus on it, taking time to really see it. Give it your full attention, examining its lines, its color, its shape, its folds, and any unique features. Notice any thoughts that come up, and simply be aware of them.

Feel it between your thumb and forefinger, exploring its texture (with your eyes closed, if you like).

Place it beneath your nose and take in the aroma, noticing any anticipatory response in your mouth or stomach.

Bring it to your lips and place it in your mouth, but don't chew it yet. Feel the sensations and taste of having it in your mouth, exploring it with your tongue. Notice if you have the urge to chew it. Be aware of anything that comes up—thoughts, anticipation, liking, disliking. Be aware of whatever you experience.

When you're ready, consciously chew once or twice, and notice what happens—notice the taste, the texture, the sensations of chewing, and anything else happening in your mouth and stomach. Take as long as you like to chew the food.

When you're ready to swallow, bring awareness to the intention to swallow, and consciously experience swallowing and digesting the food. Bring awareness to any lingering taste, the feelings of digestion, and the overall sensations in your body. If you wish, repeat this practice with another piece of food.

As you finish this practice of mindful eating, note one or two things that stood out about it. Perhaps it made it clear to you that much of the time you don't really think about what you're eating. Perhaps you realized you have a tendency to get ahead of yourself, anticipating the next bite of food before you have finished the current one. Or maybe you experienced eating in a way that was entirely new to you.

Explore bringing this mindful approach to eating one of your meals. Mindful doesn't have to mean *slow*, but slowing down can help you be more present for your experience.

Harnessing the Power of Attention— Summing Up

Focused attention is a key element of most meditation practices, not just mindfulness meditation. Focusing your attention is essential to changing unhealthy or unwanted habits, because it allows you to bring into your awareness behavioral patterns and thought patterns that were previously automatic and unconscious.

There are many different objects or "anchors" that you can use to focus your mind in meditation. One of the most commonly used and readily accessible is your own breathing. You can train your attention by bringing your awareness to the sensations of breathing and by returning your attention to your breath, with kindness and without judgment, any time you become aware that your attention has shifted.

Strengthening your faculty of attention or focus will allow you to bring awareness to an unwanted habit *before* you feel the urge to engage in it, *during* the compulsion to engage in it, and *after* you have engaged—or not engaged—in it. Bringing awareness to the habit at each of these points will help you avoid triggers, meet your urges with kind attention, and show compassion and forgiveness to yourself when you do engage in the habit.

The art of focusing your attention will help you see that whenever you're mindful, you have a choice about how to respond to what you're experiencing. And with training, you can make your default mode a present-centered awareness rather than one in which you're lost in plans, memories, or distractions—and choose to respond to urges and cravings in healthy ways that are aligned with your deepest values and intentions.

CHAPTER 7

Untangling Yourself from Habitual Thoughts and Beliefs

With our thoughts we make the world.

—Buddha

B uddhist teacher Martine Batchelor noted: "Often we are more afraid of the *idea* of something happening than the actuality of it. When we are actually confronted with it, we are able to deal adequately with the direct impact of the situation" (Batchelor 2007). This certainly fits with my own experience. When I have actually been in challenging or painful situations, I have been able to summon the resources to respond effectively, even though I feared I would be overwhelmed.

My Story

Not too long ago, I was experiencing a period of stress and anxiety. I had taken on more commitments—teaching, writing, and organizational responsibilities—than seemed possible to carry out in a way in which I was fully present for myself and others. I found myself waking in the night worried about everything that I had to do and the lack of time to do it all. It was hard to get back to sleep, because my thoughts were so insistent and anxious—*There's too much to do… How am I going to do it all?* And my difficulty falling asleep increased my anxiety—*If I'm tired and lacking energy tomorrow, it'll be even harder to get everything done*—and these anxious thoughts made sleep even more challenging. I would wake in the night with my heart beating fast. Doing some mindful walking or tai chi movements helped me relax, but not much.

It became a spiral—my worried thoughts triggered tense bodily sensations and a racing heartbeat. That spurred more intense, anxious thoughts, and in turn increased my bodily tension. And the more tense and anxious I was, the more difficult it was to relax and fall asleep.

I found myself asking, *What's the root of this problem? And what's the path to greater ease and well-being?*

I knew that mindfulness was key to finding greater peace, but it wasn't easy to simply be aware of my experience. My racing heart was sending an insistent message to my brain: *Do something; find a way out of this*, and it was really hard to sit still and observe my experience in the midst of this intensity.

Over the days and weeks that followed, I found it was helpful to investigate what I was thinking and believing about my situation and to see how identifying with my thoughts was helping perpetuate my stress and anxiety.

When I brought awareness to my thoughts and beliefs, I found that the recurring theme was *There's too much to do... I'm never going to be able to get it all done.* Underneath these thoughts was a belief that I would be letting myself and other people down if I "dropped the ball" or failed to handle my many responsibilities, and people would think less of me.

I recognized that as long as I kept treating these thoughts as true, they easily led into ever-worsening scenarios: I wouldn't be able to make a living. I would lose my home. I would lose my relationship. I would be alone. I was reminded of the Zen story of a monk in a cave who painted a tiger on the wall and became terrified each time he looked at it. I had painted my own tiger with my anxious thoughts, and I became fearful each time I got caught in my cycle of worries.

When I investigated my mental narrative of *There's too much to do*, I saw that, yes, I did have a lot to do and had taken on many commitments, but the stress and anxiety came less from all that I had to do and more from believing the narrative that I had created through my habitual thought patterns. I recalled other times when I had had many responsibilities but carried them out without anxiety because the inner *There's too much to do* narrative hadn't been present.

When I brought awareness to my thoughts and beliefs, I recognized that I had bought into a fear-based narrative that left me in a defensive state of "fight or flight." My attention and energy were exclusively focused on a defensive response. *How am I going to get all this done? How can I prevent the negative consequences of failing to get things done?* This narrow focus left very little space for making creative choices or seeing the many ways of moving forward.

As I investigated further, I saw that my worries and fears, though caused by my habitual thought patterns, were not completely "mind created." I recognized I had a tendency to say yes to requests, which came from a desire to please others and be liked by them, as well as from a wish to avoid the unpleasantness of disappointing anyone. And the growing number of yeses had led to overcommitment, which set the stage for the narrative of *There's too much to do* to feel like the truth.

As I paid wiser attention to my thoughts, it became easier to see them as thoughts rather than truths. I was able to stop buying into my mental narrative of *There's too much to do*. I could identify and note such a thought as an "anxious thought" and let it go. As I identified less with such thoughts, more space opened up for creative ways to make changes in my life—by discontinuing certain nonessential activities, by inviting others to take on roles that I didn't really need to perform myself, and by practicing saying no to requests that weren't priorities.

Much of the stress, anxiety, and suffering in our lives comes from not bringing wise attention to our thoughts and beliefs. Instead of questioning them, we treat them as true. We buy into and get swept up in the stories we tell ourselves.

Your habits play an important role in perpetuating the kinds of thoughts and beliefs that can cause you to suffer. To give you an example, if you have a habit of drinking beer to lift your mood when you feel bad, you have probably concluded *I feel better when I have a couple of beers.* An association develops in your mind between the drinking of the beers and the temporary relief that you feel, which leads you to believe you have to drink in order to feel okay. Similarly, if you have often smoked a cigarette to avoid feeling sad or lonely, you have probably come to the conclusion that you'll feel sad or lonely if you don't smoke a cigarette. As psychologist Donald Hebb observed more than sixty years ago, neurons that fire together wire together (Hebb 1949). Your mind associates the behavior (drinking beer, smoking a cigarette) with a reprieve from the unpleasant feelings, and as a result you generate thoughts that reinforce the behavior.

Bringing mindfulness to your thoughts is essential if you hope to loosen your identification with negative patterns of thinking. If you look at the four different kinds of habits— habits of wanting, habits of resisting, habits of distraction, and habits of doing—you can see the patterns of thoughts and beliefs that most often underpin and fuel them. Any time you're caught up in unhealthy habits of *wanting*—craving food, drink, tobacco, sex, recognition—the underlying thought is typically *I'll feel better, if only I can have* _____ . And underlying this wanting is the belief *Things will be painful or unpleasant if I can't have* _____ . Habits of *resisting* or *aversion*—in which you express frustration, anger, impatience, and harsh judgments—tend to have the underlying thought *This needs to be different for me to feel okay.* Or *If I don't change this, something really bad will happen.* With habits of *distraction*—such as constantly checking your phone or spending excessive time watching TV—the underlying thinking is typically that your present experience is boring or unpleasant and that doing something familiar will be more interesting or enjoyable. Habits of *doing*—when your energies are always focused on the next thing you need to get done—tend to have the underlying thought *Something bad will happen if I don't keep moving.* All of these habits are accompanied by an underlying belief that the present moment is insufficient. *I'll only be happy if this changes, or if I have that...or if I get these things done.*

Mindfulness practice can loosen your identification with thoughts, helping you see that the content of a thought is not inherently true. If you can pay closer attention to your thoughts, you'll act on those thoughts more wisely, rather than in habitual ways. For example, when discomfort, loneliness, or boredom triggers the thought *Some ice cream would be nice now,* you can observe this as "wanting" or "wanting thought," rather than automatically going to the freezer and scooping yourself a bowl of ice cream.

You can deepen your awareness of the emotions and bodily sensations that often underlie and spur your habitual thought patterns and behavioral patterns. And if you have beliefs that perpetuate unhealthy habits, you can investigate these beliefs and untangle yourself from them. Following are three approaches for working with thoughts and beliefs.

Observing Your Thoughts, Letting Them Come and Go

One of the most powerful realizations that you can come to in mindfulness practice is to see that you can bring awareness to your thoughts and beliefs rather than being lost in them or ruled by them. There's all the difference in the world between, on one hand, *bringing awareness* to feeling angry at something a colleague said—feeling the tension and heat in your face and chest, paying attention to and observing your feelings of annoyance and your thoughts of what you might say—and, on the other hand, *being swept up* in the anger and the accompanying mental narrative of how mean or wrong your colleague is or what you'll say to him.

If you bring awareness to your thoughts—including your opinions, ideas, and beliefs—you can determine how to behave wisely and appropriately. Choices will open up for you—including the choice not to believe or identify with your thoughts. If you fail to bring awareness to your thoughts, however, you'll have little choice but to act out old thought patterns and follow them. The unexamined thought *A bowl of ice cream would be nice right now* can lead you to the freezer before you know you have made a choice. A story often used to illustrate this point goes like this: A horse and rider are galloping along at great speed when a bystander shouts out, "Where are you going?" and the rider responds, "Don't ask me—ask the horse!" Much of the time, your horse, in the form of your habitual, unexamined thoughts, decides where you go.

So, an essential mindfulness skill is to develop a healthy relationship with your thoughts—seeing thoughts as ephemeral products of your mind rather than as *the truth*. Whenever you practice mindfulness of breathing, or mindfulness of some other object of awareness, you may notice that your attention is frequently drawn away by your thoughts. You may get caught up in planning, worrying, daydreaming, or remembering the past. When you become aware that your attention has shifted to your thoughts, it can be helpful to make a mental note (as mentioned in practice 7, "Mindfulness of Breathing Meditation"), such as *thinking, planning, daydreaming,* or *worried thought*. The practice of naming your thoughts or noting *thinking* can help you observe thoughts as passing phenomena, rather than getting lost in the content of those thoughts.

An attitude of kindness and nonjudgment will help you develop a healthy relationship with your thoughts; there's no need to try to get rid of thoughts or empty your mind, even during meditation. If you have thoughts that you consider to be problematic in any way, this is an indication that your relationship with those thoughts calls for wise attention. If you can experience your thoughts without resistance, clinging, or judgment, those thoughts will cease to be a problem.

Seeing your thoughts as only thoughts, and choosing to come back to the present by letting go of your mental narratives, will help you loosen your identification with the thoughts and beliefs that can keep you locked in unhealthy habits.

Untangling Your Thoughts from Your Bodily Sensations and Emotions

Bringing awareness to your present-moment experience and returning your attention to your "anchor" when you become aware that you have drifted into thought is an essential mindfulness skill.

At times, however, your thoughts are tied to sensations, emotions, and urges that can perpetuate unhealthy habits if you don't bring awareness to them as well. For example, a wistful memory might bring on sadness and a feeling of heaviness in your heart and around your eyes, and these feelings might trigger an urge to space out by going online—particularly if this is an established pattern for you. You might find yourself going from site to site on the Internet without a clear purpose or any awareness that you have consciously made a choice to "check out." This habit doesn't serve you.

But if you allow yourself to experience the sensations, emotions, and urges that accompany your thoughts, you can untangle the complex web of your inner experiences and choose to act in ways that do serve your deeper happiness and well-being. You can explore this practice of *untangling* in formal meditation periods, and it'll support awareness of your habit urges as they arise in your daily life.

If you're using your breath as your meditation object or "anchor," you can simply return your attention to your breathing when you become aware that you have been lost in thought. However, if you find that you keep being pulled back to a recurrent thought—for example, a painful memory or a fearful or anxious thought—then, rather than simply returning your attention to your breath, bring awareness to whatever sensations or emotions are present in your body. If there's tightness in your chest or belly, be fully open to those sensations. Direct your attention to the location of the painful or uncomfortable sensations, and, as you do so, breathe in a deep and relaxed way so that the difficult feelings are being held, as it were, by your relaxed breathing (this is known as *breathing into* the sensations, as if you're breathing directly into specific parts of your body). Breathe into the sensations, meeting them with kindness and acceptance, and let them go in their own time. If it's helpful, note *tightness* or *tension* or *heat* or *numbness*. Be open to whatever emotions are present, making a note (for example, *anger*) if it's helpful. If worried, sad, or fearful thoughts arise, simply bring awareness to them, noting *thinking* or *sad thought*.

Let each part of your experience be simply what it is—allow thoughts to be thoughts, allow emotions to be emotions, and allow sensations to be sensations, each coming and going in its own time.

Investigating Beliefs and Narratives

If you're used to thinking and acting in particular ways, over time you may come to believe that you don't have any choice in relation to these thoughts or actions. You may even believe *This is who I am.*

If you have developed a habit of responding angrily to small annoyances or slights, you may easily believe *I'm an angry person* or *People are stupid* and think that you have no choice but to get angry when someone does or says something that rubs you the wrong way.

If you have smoked cigarettes for many years, you may believe *I'm a smoker* or *I don't have the willpower to quit*—and these beliefs can help keep you addicted to cigarettes.

If you aimlessly surf the web for the first hour of work, you may believe *I'll never be productive at work* and that you can't be mindful when you sit down at your desk in the morning.

If you're in a constant state of stress, rushing to get everything done, you might believe *I'm never going to be able to keep up* or *Things are never going to change.* And this belief helps fuel your stressful state.

It's important to investigate such beliefs and narratives and to see the ways in which you're identifying with them. Seeing that these narratives are a creation of your mind rather than absolute truth can allow you to untangle yourself from them so that they cease to fuel unhealthy patterns of thought and behavior.

You can begin by asking yourself, *Is this really true? Is it true that "I'm an angry person" or "I don't have the willpower to quit" or "I'll never be able to get all these things done"? Or is this a mental narrative that I have developed and identified with over time and which, as such, is not concrete, is not "me," and can be let go of?*

You can counter negative beliefs and narratives (which often feature the word "never" or "always," as shown above) with examples that call your mental narrative into question. For instance, if the belief underlying your unwanted habit is *I'm indecisive and unfocused*, you might recall a Saturday morning when you were up early and focused for a long hike in the mountains.

A meditation that can help you work with deeply entrenched beliefs is known by the acronym RAIN (Recognizing, Allowing, Investigating, and Not identifying). This meditation can help you dissolve deep-seated beliefs about yourself and your limitations. The version below is influenced by Tara Brach's teachings of RAIN and builds on the work of Byron Katie (Brach 2013; Katie 2002). In this practice, first, you bring to mind an unhealthy habit. Then you *recognize* what's present in your body, emotions, and thoughts and *allow* it to be just as it is—to come and go in its own time. Then, the more you *investigate* the beliefs and narratives that perpetuate the habit, the more you can *not identify* with them and abandon them.

Practice 10: RAIN Meditation on an Unwanted or Unhealthy Habit

Sit in a comfortable, relaxed posture with your back straight and your shoulders relaxed. Take a few moments to settle your body and mind as you take some deep breaths, and on each out-breath letting go of any tension or stress you might be holding.

Then, with a relaxed attention, be open to whatever is present. Meet it with kindness, curiosity, and acceptance.

When you're ready, consciously bring to mind an unhealthy or unwanted habit that you wish to investigate. As you think about this habit, turn your awareness to your bodily sensations. Notice what's present. If there's tightness in your chest, or your face is hot, for example, be fully open to these sensations. Be interested in them. Notice how they come, how they stay for a time, how they change (if they do), and then how they pass. If it helps you be accepting, inwardly say yes to whatever you experience: yes to tightness…yes to numbness…yes to heat. Allow each sensation to be as it is, to come and go in its own time.

Meet any emotions in the same way—naming them, if this is helpful—for example, *shame, anger, grief*—and say yes to these emotions, allowing them to come and go in their own time.

Bring awareness, too, to any thoughts, beliefs, or narratives that are present. For example, *I'll never be able to change this, Nothing ever works out for me,* or *I'm a loser—I have no self-control.* Hold these thoughts and beliefs in your awareness with kindness, saying yes to their presence.

As you sit with the sensations, emotions, and thoughts that are present, ask yourself, *What am I believing about this situation?* You might notice the thought *No one really cares about me* or *Nothing's going to change* or *I'm always going to be alone,* accompanied by a sinking feeling in your heart and the urge to comfort yourself in a familiar but unhealthy way. Meet these feelings and beliefs with kindness and care. Examine one belief at a time, asking yourself, *Is this really true?* As you sit with this question, situations that counter the belief may come to mind— for example, memories showing that people do care about you. If your belief is a negative belief about the future, remember that no one can predict the future with 100 percent accuracy, because the future is unknowable. Reflect on the fact that it's impossible to know how events will unfold.

Ask yourself, *What's it like to live with this belief?* Has this belief served you? Does it enhance your well-being, or does it lead to suffering? How has it affected your life? Has it narrowed your options? Cut you off from friends, family, yourself? What sensations and emotions go with this belief—a feeling of heaviness? A feeling of being small? Disappointment? Sadness? Say yes to the feelings while continuing to investigate the belief.

Inquire further into the belief, asking yourself, *What's preventing me from letting go of this belief?* You might find that beneath the belief is fear. Perhaps you fear that letting go of the belief will leave you vulnerable, that something bad might happen. Holding on to the belief may provide a sense of control or self-protection. Be as fully open as you can to the feelings beneath the belief. You might place your hand on your heart and ask these feelings—of tightness, or fear, for example—*What do you need or want from me?* Open to whatever response arises—it might be *kindness*, or *acceptance*, or *love*. Meet whatever arises with kindness and care.

As you continue to closely investigate this belief—and the sensations and emotions that accompany it—ask yourself, *How would it be to live without this belief?* Imagine living without this limiting belief affecting your body, heart, and mind. Imagine you have let go of this belief, and bring awareness to how that feels. You might experience a sense of relief or of spaciousness. Or it may be hard to even imagine letting go of the belief. Keep investigating with kindness: *How would it be to live without this belief? And who would I be without this belief?*

It may feel unsettling to lose your sense of certainty about who you are and what will happen as you explore the possibility of living without this limiting belief. This is a normal part of the process of non-identification with your beliefs. Keep in mind that the less sure you are about yourself and the world, the more opportunities are available to you in any given moment.

As a simple mindfulness practice, any time you're drawn toward an unhealthy habit, ask yourself: *What am I believing right now? Do I believe that I need to* _____ (for example, have sex, watch TV, or drive aggressively) *to be happy or to feel okay? If so, what would it be like to live without this belief? Or do I believe that I need to* _____ *to get rid of a certain thought? If so, can I experience this thought as simply a thought, label it* (for example, "anxious thought" or "angry thought"), *and let it pass? Or do I believe that I need to* _____ *to get rid of a certain emotion? If so, can I experience this emotion as simply an emotion, label it* (for example, "boredom" or "sadness"), *and let it pass? Finally, Can I choose to bring my awareness back to my breath or body?*

Untangling Yourself from Habitual Thoughts and Beliefs—Summing Up

Beliefs that justify and perpetuate unhealthy habits tend to become stronger over time. It's a vicious cycle: The repetition of the habit helps strengthen the belief that you have to engage in the habit to feel okay, which further fuels the habit. Over time, your habits and beliefs can become so strong that they seem to be simply part of who you are.

The mindfulness practices in this book provide ways of working with thoughts and beliefs and letting go of beliefs that keep you mired in unhealthy habits.

First, the practice of bringing awareness to your thoughts and choosing to bring your attention back to your breath (or some other "anchor") will help loosen your identification with thoughts and develop a more healthy relationship with them. You'll begin to see your thoughts as simply thoughts, not necessarily truths.

Second, mindfulness practices will help you untangle your thoughts and beliefs from your sensations, feelings, and emotions, so that certain sensations don't automatically trigger painful thoughts and beliefs, and vice versa.

Finally, you can investigate your beliefs that help perpetuate unhealthy habits. You can ask yourself:

- *What am I believing?*

- *Is this really true?*

- *How is it to live with this belief?*

- *How would it be to live without this belief?*

- *Who would I be without this belief?*

Working with your thoughts through these practices of mindfulness and inquiry will weaken any long-standing beliefs that fuel and perpetuate unhealthy habits, enabling you to live more freely.

CHAPTER 8

Riding the Waves of Emotions, Urges, and Cravings

You can't control the waves, but you can learn to surf.

—Zen saying

To be mindful is to take refuge in reality by being open to your experience without resistance, judgment, or clinging. Any time you meet your experience wholeheartedly, with kindness and acceptance, you're in alignment with the flow of your life as it unfolds here and now. But any time you let your thoughts, worries, and stresses dictate how you experience this moment, you inevitably suffer, because you're in conflict with reality, with truth. Rather than dancing with life, you're in a wrestling match—and the outcome of the struggle isn't in doubt.

This moment may be an extremely painful one. Your bodily sensations might be urging you to find comfort or release in food, drink, drugs, sex, or some other craving. Your thoughts might be telling you you must have this thing, or person, or experience, otherwise life will be intolerable. Or you might be experiencing intense pain of loss, worry about the future, or physical pain. But even in these intense situations, mindfulness provides a path out of craving, stress, and suffering. The way out is by going through the experience, being fully open to all its dimensions—feelings, sensations, emotions, thoughts, cravings, urges—and seeing that all these eventually pass.

In the previous chapter, I related my experience of working with anxiety and how my thoughts and beliefs helped perpetuate the painful emotions. As mentioned, examining and letting go of certain thoughts and beliefs helped me reduce my stress and anxiety. But the other key to freedom from the habit of anxious thinking was being fully open to the experience and saying yes to whatever was present—being willing to feel the unpleasant bodily sensations (such as muscle tension and a racing heart) and emotions (such as worry and fear) that accompanied and underlay the anxious thoughts.

My Story—Continued

Any time I was caught up in a state of anxiety, I felt that something bad was happening to me and that I needed to do something to make it go away. The more I resisted my anxiety, the more time I spent locked in struggle. One night, when I awoke and couldn't get back to sleep, I resolved to do something different. I decided, *I'm going to let myself feel whatever I'm feeling without resistance.* Over the next forty-five minutes or so, I paid close attention to the fears and anxieties as they welled up in my body. I felt my heart pounding like a drum, and I said yes to my pounding heart. I felt the tension in my stomach, chest, and throat, and I breathed into it and felt it soften a little. I was aware of thoughts of *There's too much to do*, and I let them go. I practiced riding the waves of sensations and emotions, and I said yes to each wave. The more I was open to the waves of sensations, feelings, and emotions, the more they felt simply like waves of experience—more impersonal, less about *me* and more like a common human reaction to pressure and stress. As each wave passed, I experienced a period of ease before the arrival of the next wave. And as time went on and I kept saying yes to my direct experience, the waves settled and I rested in a state of deep peace and well-being.

In the preceding chapters, I presented skills and practices that can help you be open to your experience—by clarifying your intentions, saying yes to your experience, developing wise attention, and cultivating attitudes of heart and mind that support mindful awareness. In this chapter, we'll discuss ways of bringing mindfulness to experiences that are particularly challenging and intense.

The practices of mindfulness in this book invite you to be open to your experience—the joys and the sorrows—and experience the freedom and well-being that come from being fully open to life, rather than escaping into habits to avoid unpleasantness.

But how do you work with emotions, cravings, and urges that are so strong that your brain is saying "hell, no" to staying with your experience? For example, how can mindfulness help you respond wisely and kindly in the following situations?

You're walking down a quiet street, enjoying the sunshine, when suddenly a car backfires loudly. You're a war veteran, and your instinct is to react as if you were under fire. Even though you know you're no longer in a combat zone, your "survival brain" is panicking: *Do something! Get out of here!*

You're in recovery from drug or alcohol addiction, or you have recently quit smoking, and you're feeling an intense craving. You know that acting on the urge will be harmful and strengthen the habit or addiction, and yet you find it very hard to resist.

You're in a tense conversation with a family member or friend, when he says something that pushes a familiar button in you. You feel defensive and have a sudden urge to lash out verbally.

Any time a wanting or craving is triggered (by a specific environment, a particular time or place, or certain feelings), your brain sends you the message *I have to have _____ to feel better* or *Things will be terrible if I don't have _____* .

Through habit, over time, you have come to associate getting or having what you crave with feeling okay, even if you know deep down that the craving leads to suffering and that getting what you want won't provide true happiness. Your primitive "survival brain," which we discussed in chapter 2, is sending you an urgent message to take action. And the wiser message from your prefrontal cortex, *This is not healthy or helpful*, will feel less compelling and can be overridden if you're not paying attention. What Walter Mischel calls the "hot" brain system can easily overpower the "cool," the slower and rational process (Mischel 2014).

Similarly, if you feel a strong emotion—fear, for example—the message from your survival brain is typically to do something—fight, flee, or freeze—rather than open yourself to the feeling. So, for example, if you have a habit of becoming fearful any time you feel as if the world is making too many demands on you, when that emotion arises it may be difficult for you to observe it as simply an impersonal energy that comes and goes.

A mindfulness practice that can support you in working with strong emotions and urges is learning to ride the waves of your experience (also known as "surfing the urge"). This practice involves understanding the temporary nature of emotions and mind states and learning to open yourself to the many aspects of your direct experience—your sensations, emotions, thoughts, and desires—without acting on them.

It can be difficult to experience a strong craving or emotion without either acting on it or repressing it. Sometimes the reason for this is a belief that if you don't do *something*, the feeling will last forever. As overwhelming as the craving or emotion may seem, this simply is not true. Unlike moods, which can continue for hours, emotions are "more in the realm of minutes and seconds" (Ekman 1994, 56). If you understand that emotions—as well as thoughts, urges, and sensations—stay for only a while, this can encourage you to let yourself experience them.

The poet Anne Morrow Lindbergh has said of physical pain:

> Go with the pain, let it take you… Open your palms and your body to the pain. It comes in waves like a tide, and you must be open as a vessel lying on the beach, letting it fill you up and then, retreating, leaving you empty and clear. With a deep breath—it

has to be as deep as the pain—one reaches a kind of inner freedom from pain, as though the pain were not yours but your body's. The spirit lays the body on the altar. (Cited in Kornfield 2008, 114)

Sarah's Story

Sarah was a student in one of my mindfulness-based stress reduction (MBSR) classes. She told us of how one day, as she was settling into a meditation practice and bringing attention to her body, she got a tingling sensation on her skin that was oddly similar to a sensation that she associated with panic. In fact, the tingling seemed to be triggering feelings of panic.

She had experienced a full-blown panic attack only once before, but she remembered enough from that experience and its aftermath to recognize what was happening. So she used some mindfulness practices to help her get through the next few minutes. "I watched my mind and body as the symptoms of panic attack set in. I consciously slowed my breath and brought a smile to my lips. I breathed and watched for maybe fifteen or thirty seconds, saying to myself, *These are just thoughts and feelings.* Then I said, *I am feeling panicky, but my awareness is not panicking.* I wasn't just giving myself a pep talk; it was true. Whatever was watching this panic attack was doing so from a place of calm. With that statement, I chose to identify with the awareness rather than the panic." As a result of that realization, the panic attack subsided quickly and Sarah felt a sense of triumph and relief.

The experience returned at other times that day and over the subsequent months. Each time, the anxiety subsided as Sarah held it in her awareness, just as it had the first time. At times, she would avoid meditating, afraid that the anxiety would appear unannounced. But then she remembered that in meditation, since you're sitting and watching your mind, there's less opportunity for something to just "sneak up on you."

The key to riding the waves of a challenging experience is to rest in the awareness that, as Sarah described it, is watching the experience (the panic, fear, anger, craving, or other difficult feeling) from "a place of calm." The awareness is not panicking or fearful but is observing the feelings that we call "panic" or "fear." To find freedom and peace amid the storms and turbulence in your life, remember that the waves (of emotion, craving, and so forth) are impermanent. They're not a part of you; they're impersonal energies that come and go. You can work with them and find freedom through resting in your awareness and engaging in practices that help you ride the waves.

You can use the following meditation when working with a strong craving or other difficult urges or emotions.

Practice 11: Riding the Waves of Intense Experience

Find a comfortable, relaxed sitting posture, with your back straight, your shoulders relaxed, and your eyes gently closed. Or, if you prefer to keep your eyes open, look ahead with a soft, unfocused gaze.

Take a few deep breaths, inviting a calming of your body and mind as you breathe in and a release of tension as you breathe out.

Bring your awareness into your body. Moving your attention down your body, invite any area of tension—facial muscles, eyes, shoulders, chest, belly—to relax.

Sit in a way that's relaxed and alert.

Bring to mind a time when you felt a strong urge or craving for something that you knew wasn't healthy or a wise choice. Or recall a time when you experienced a strong emotion that felt difficult or painful. (Start with a situation that was moderately challenging, rather than one that was very intense.) Be open to whatever you're experiencing; commit to staying with your direct feelings, rather than pushing them away or acting out the urge, emotion, or craving.

Bring awareness to your bodily sensations, and feel what's present. For example, if there's tightness or tension in your chest, open yourself to it and breathe into the feelings; say yes to them—saying Yes in your mind, if that's helpful. Pay close attention to the feelings, and notice whether they change. Do they get stronger or weaker? Do they go away for a time? Do they metamorphose into other kinds of feelings? For example, does tightness slowly turn into pulsing or throbbing? Can you experience these sensations as waves that build up, crest, and then subside?

Bring the same kind and accepting attention to the energies of strong emotions—fear, sadness, anger—or feelings of wanting. Recognize how these energies also come and go, rise and fall, crest and subside, often bringing with them strong urges that you might typically respond to by acting on the urge or resisting a painful emotion. If it's helpful, visualize the intense urges, cravings, or emotions as waves, and see yourself riding the waves.

Bring awareness to your thoughts, and see how these too come and go if you don't act on them. Continue to ride the waves of these challenging experiences—saying yes to whatever arises. You can continue this practice for a set time, say ten or fifteen minutes, or, if you prefer, continue until you feel ready to end the meditation. Then, open your eyes and bring your attention back to your surroundings.

You can also ride the waves of craving or challenging emotions any time you're in the midst of a difficult or painful experience, if you can pause whatever you're doing and take some quiet moments to open yourself to your direct experience in the way outlined here.

The following meditation practice is derived from Somatic Experiencing (SE), a mind-body approach to healing trauma developed by Peter Levine (Levine 1997). This meditation can be particularly helpful any time you're working with experiences that feel too painful or intense to stay with. The SE approach—of which this is just one important element—provides skillful ways of opening to intense experiences as they manifest in your body but shifting your awareness to an experience of greater peace, calm, or well-being before they become overwhelming. The key is to consciously shift your attention to a "resource"—a place of ease, safety, or greater peace, such as a pleasant bodily sensation, a positive memory, or an image of a loved one—and then, from that space of greater balance and resilience, gently bring your awareness back to the intense experience. Gently moving your attention back and forth (called "pendulation" in Somatic Experiencing) between the "resource" and the challenging experience can help release stored energies of trauma that get locked in your body. This can also be a helpful practice for working with other nontraumatic but intense experiences.

Practice 12: Touching In and Touching Out of Intense Experiences

Begin this meditation in the same way as the "riding the waves" meditation by taking some time to arrive and settle into a comfortable posture, relaxed and alert.

Take a few moments to bring to mind something in your life or your direct experience that feels like a source of support or a refuge—something or someone it gives you a feeling of peace, connectedness, strength, or well-being to think of. It could be a place you used to go on vacation that brings back loving and peaceful memories; a beloved family member, friend, mentor, or pet; your spiritual beliefs or practices; or anything that gives you a feeling of peace, well-being, or support. Let yourself experience how it feels in your body and emotions to bring this special person or experience (referred to in therapy as a "resource") to mind. Feel yourself held and supported. If it's difficult to find a positive resource, try to locate a neutral feeling—for example, sensations in your feet, seat, or hands.

If there's something painful or difficult that you're currently dealing with that arouses intense or painful feelings, invite the feelings into your consciousness in a kind and friendly way, then let your awareness come into your body. What do you feel in your body? Where do you feel it? If you feel tightness in your chest and throat, be fully open to these sensations. Imagine their details: Do they have a shape, a color, a texture? What's the area around these tight feelings like? Explore your bodily sensations, offering a kind and curious attention to them. Notice how they change and move, how they come and go. Do the same for your emotions and thoughts. You may find that when you bring kind and intimate attention to the painful or difficult experience, the difficult feelings come and then go in their own time.

If, however, the experience becomes intense and it's too difficult or painful to stay focused on your bodily sensations, emotions, or thoughts, gently think of your "resource" and rest in the sense of ease, peace, well-being, or connection that arises when you do so. Stay with these feelings as long as necessary to bring yourself back into balance. Then, when you're ready, gently return your attention to the intense experience. Notice how it feels as you bring your attention back to the place of difficulty, and bring awareness to what, if anything, has changed. Find the place where the feelings were most intense, and hold it within the feeling of peace, resilience, or well-being. Do this for fifteen minutes or until the end of your meditation period.

You can use this practice of moving gently back and forth between the intense experience and your "resource" as a way of opening yourself fully to the underlying energies that are triggering the strong feelings, then allowing them to dissipate. You can also use this practice any time challenging or intense experiences arise unbidden in meditation or in daily life.

Riding the Waves of Emotions, Urges, and Cravings—Summing Up

Any time you intentionally bring awareness to your direct experience with kindness, curiosity, and acceptance, your experience changes. As the spiritual teacher Krishnamurti said, "If you begin to understand what you are without trying to change it, then what you are undergoes a transformation" (Krishnamurti, n.d.).

At times, however, you may encounter feelings that are very difficult to be open to—panic, fear, strong cravings or addictions, or painful emotions. Specific mindfulness practices can be very helpful in building the skills to work with these intense situations.

The Here-and-Now Habit

A key to transforming intense experiences is learning that you're not your bodily experiences, your emotions, your cravings, or your thoughts. For example, rather than being angry (and being caught up in the story of what led you to be angry), you can be aware of your anger; rather than being sad, you can be aware of your sadness. You can observe your experience without becoming swept up in it or completely identified with it.

If you can learn to "ride the waves" of the intense experience, being open to the sensations, emotions, and thoughts that accompany it, you'll see that even the most challenging moments have a limited life span. They come, stay for a time, and then pass. This realization can bring you great freedom and peace.

CHAPTER 9

Taking In the Good: Cultivating Emotions That Support Well-Being and Happiness

May all beings be happy.
May they live in safety and joy.

—Buddha

When you want to meet a need for comfort, safety, or well-being, or to avoid an unpleasant feeling, such as fear, loneliness, or sadness, you find the best available means of assuaging the difficult feelings or getting what you think you need. You may take refuge in alcohol, drugs, cigarettes, shopping, sexual activity, online browsing, or myriad other ways of finding short-term relief. As you know by now, if you do this behavior repeatedly and under similar circumstances, it may turn into an unhealthy habit. Habits are difficult to change, but mindful awareness can be a vital path to abandoning unwanted habits and developing more beneficial ones.

Another skill that helps bring your life into harmony with your values and intentions is the cultivation of beneficial emotions and states of mind. These include contentment, joy, peace, compassion, and loving-kindness, all of which are conducive to your well-being and help limit the impact of afflictive emotions and mind states.

Throughout this book, I have approached emotions not as inherently "good" or "bad," "positive" or "negative," but rather as natural responses to conditions and situations whose impact depends on how you meet them. So, although people often think of anger as a negative emotion, if you meet the energy of your anger with mindfulness and self-compassion, it doesn't need to have a negative effect; it can simply come and go like a powerful weather system passing through. Anger can also be a call to appropriate action—for instance, when you respond wisely and with compassion to an injustice that you witness. The same is true of other challenging emotions, such as shame, guilt, sadness, and fear.

Conversely, emotions we think of as positive can have painful consequences if not met with mindfulness and wisdom. Joy can become mindless exuberance. Love without awareness can lead to craving or unhealthy attachment. Equanimity can become indifference or disconnection.

Emotions are signals to respond to events or situations (or your own thinking). So-called negative emotions, which have their origins in millions of years of evolution, were crucial to the survival of our ancestors (Hutson 2015). Fear, which arises in response to perceived threats, activates your body and mind to escape danger or protect yourself. Anger motivates you to take action to protect your welfare. Shame and guilt spur you to be conscious of your situation and your actions and to respond appropriately.

Fear, anger, shame, and guilt are thus extremely valuable when taken as helpful signals. But when you respond to these challenging emotions in unskillful ways, the consequences can be negative even if the emotions themselves are not. So, if someone acts in a way that makes you angry and you respond with a narrative about what a terrible person he is, perhaps compounding that story with fears about other harmful things he might do, you may justify harming him to protect yourself. We see this throughout history wherever groups and leaders have called for attacking others as a way of responding to fears, unleashing great avoidable suffering.

A frightening situation that metamorphoses into a story in your mind that the same thing might happen again can lead to chronic anxiety or post-traumatic stress. Guilt or shame can lead to powerlessness, depression, or self-harm, if you don't meet it mindfully. The key lies in how you respond.

One important difference between emotions that are often called "negative" (fear, anger, shame, sadness) and those typically referred to as "positive" (for example, joy, love, and contentment) is that the former narrow your focus, whereas the latter broaden your range of options. Consciously inviting into your awareness emotions that expand your range of options can help you work skillfully with challenging emotions that narrow your focus. This is particularly the case when you're working with anger, sadness, and fear, which often trigger unhealthy or harmful habits.

Barbara Fredrickson, a psychologist at the University of North Carolina and an expert in the field of positive psychology, has demonstrated this principle in her lab. Though I don't share her use of the terms "positive" and "negative" to describe emotions (for reasons already discussed), the research is compelling, and I'll retain her terms while discussing it.

Fredrickson and her colleagues showed, in studies, that activating positive emotions allowed individuals to undo the cardiovascular effects of negative emotions. In one study, participants were shown a film clip that elicited fear and brought about increased cardiovascular activity (measured by heart rate, blood pressure, and other measures). Participants who then watched a second film clip meant to elicit a positive emotion (as opposed to a film clip meant to elicit sadness or a film clip meant to elicit no emotion) showed the fastest cardiovascular recovery, supporting the hypothesis that positive emotions undo negative emotions (Fredrickson and Levenson 1998).

Fredrickson concludes that cultivating positive emotions can counter the narrowing effect of negative emotions. Positive and negative emotions are fundamentally incompatible. As she describes it, an individual's "thought-action repertoire" cannot be both narrow and broad at the same time, and this incompatibility accounts for the undoing effect of positive emotions (Fredrickson 2000).

The implications of the work of Fredrickson and her colleagues are significant for transforming harmful habits. Very often when we're experiencing a painful emotion, mood, or mind state, we gravitate toward unhealthy patterns of behavior. When you're feeling sad, lonely, angry, or afraid, it's very easy to reach for the easiest or most accessible way to comfort yourself, but usually this won't be what's best for you in the long term or reflect your deepest intentions.

Buddhist teachings support what Fredrickson discovered in her lab. For example, cultivating loving-kindness is an antidote to anger and hatred, and inspiration is an antidote to doubt. Here are some ways you can respond to challenging emotions and mind states with emotions that broaden your options:

- If you're feeling *bored* or *numb*—and may be susceptible to distracting yourself by spending large amounts of time online—begin by opening fully to the experience of "boredom": How does it feel in your body? What are the thoughts and beliefs going through your mind? Meet your experience with genuine acceptance, recognizing what's present and allowing it to be just as it is. Then, invite an attitude of *interest* and *curiosity* toward the challenging feelings and toward your experience as a whole. Incline your mind toward interest, investigation, and curiosity, and see how your experience unfolds.

- If you're *restless* or *agitated* and feel pulled into a habitual mode of "doing," moving toward the future, or soothing these uncomfortable feelings in an unhealthy way, open yourself with full acceptance to what you're feeling. Then, when you're ready, bring to mind an image of *peace*. Remember a time you felt calm and at ease, and send a wish of peace or ease to yourself: *May I be peaceful…may I live with ease.* Cultivate peace or calm as an antidote to restlessness or agitation.

- If you're feeling *sad* or *blue* and pulled toward habitual eating, drinking, or distracting yourself, meet these feelings and associated thoughts with kindness and acceptance. Then, when you're ready, invite into your heart and mind feelings of *joy* and *happiness*. You might bring to mind a time when you felt happy and joyful. You might think about someone who evokes these feelings in you or reflect on everything in your life that you're grateful for. Allow these joyful feelings to arise naturally.

- If you feel *angry* or *fearful* and sense the urge to say or do something harmful to yourself or another, or to soothe yourself in an unhealthy way, meet the feelings of anger or fear with kindness and acceptance. Then, when you feel ready, incline your mind toward *loving-kindness* or *compassion*. If you're reacting to something unkind or thoughtless that a friend or family member has said or done, first, meet your own experience with kindness and compassion. Acknowledge the pain you're experiencing by putting your hand on your heart and saying, "I care about this suffering," or send a compassionate wish to yourself, such as "May I be free from pain and suffering." If and when you feel ready, you can reflect on the other person's wish to be happy, consider the conditions in her life that might have given rise to her unkind or thoughtless behavior, then wish her well: "May you be free from pain and suffering," "May you be happy." Continue this practice for as long as it feels helpful.

One of the most important things to bear in mind when cultivating beneficial and expansive emotions as an antidote to painful feelings or mind states is that you're not doing it to avoid, resist, deny, or in any way escape from the difficult feelings. Resisting your experience paves the way for difficult emotions and mind states to persist. Bringing emotions like joy and contentment to painful feelings such as fear and anger is more akin to creating a surrounding space of peace, tranquility, kindness, or love in which you can hold the difficult feeling or allow it to dissolve.

We'll now explore two long-established practices that have been shown in recent scientific studies to lessen people's stress and anxiety and improve their well-being and quality of life. These practices are loving-kindness and self-compassion.

Loving-Kindness

The practice of loving-kindness has its origins in the teachings of the Buddha as a way to mitigate fear and anger, as well as cultivate feelings of friendliness, kindness, and happiness toward all beings. In the Buddhist story of the origins of loving-kindness meditation, a group of monks went to the forest to meditate. The spirits of the forest resented their intrusion and emitted fearful sounds and odious smells that greatly disconcerted the monks, who went to the Buddha and asked for a more serene place to meditate. The Buddha said no, but he taught them the practice of loving-kindness. When the monks went back to the forest, the spirits felt their love and friendliness and welcomed and protected them.

Sharon Salzberg, a leading meditation teacher, commented on this story of the origins of loving-kindness practice: "The inner meaning of the story is that a mind filled with fear can still be penetrated by the quality of lovingkindness. Moreover, a mind that is saturated by lovingkindness cannot be overcome by fear; even if fear should arise, it will not overpower such a mind" (Salzberg 1995, 21).

Loving-kindness is a quality that is described as "boundless" and "immeasurable" because, with training, there's no limit to the kindness and love you can feel for yourself and others and no boundary to those whom you can include in your wishes and intentions.

Loving-kindness is one of four qualities that in Buddhism are called "divine abodes"—or our natural and best home. The other qualities are *compassion*—the response of an open and loving heart to the suffering of another or oneself; *sympathetic* or *appreciative joy*—being happy in another's happiness; and *equanimity*—evenness and balance of mind in the face of pain and pleasure, joys and sorrows, and all life's vicissitudes.

These open-hearted qualities arise naturally when painful or afflictive mind states aren't present. When you abandon painful states like anger and greed, you'll open to your natural goodness and loving nature. You can also cultivate these qualities by consciously wishing yourself and others well.

The practice involves intentionally wishing for the well-being of all sentient beings, expressed in phrases such as "May I/you/all beings be safe…happy…healthy." Traditionally, the practice begins with sending wishes of safety, happiness, and well-being toward yourself—"May I be happy"—since it's very difficult to genuinely wish others happiness if you're closed and judgmental toward yourself. You then include dear friends and loved ones, neutral people, difficult people, and ultimately all sentient beings. Through opening your heart to those to whom it's easiest to feel kind and loving, you can build your capacity to wish well to more difficult people in your life.

You can use words, images, and feelings to invite qualities of kindness and friendliness to arise in you. However, you don't need to feel kind or loving as you do this practice; it's enough to have the intention to wish well to yourself and others. In doing so, you're planting seeds of kindness and love, but you can't predict when they'll blossom. And if negative feelings come up—for example, annoyance, frustration, or anger—meet them with kindness and continue sending wishes of friendliness.

Practice 13: Loving-Kindness Meditation

Begin by finding a comfortable and relaxed posture, whether in a chair, on a cushion or bench, or lying down. Let go of plans and memories you may be contemplating, and allow yourself to be here. Take two or three deep breaths, feeling your breath moving through your chest and the area of your heart.

Begin with yourself: silently repeat the following phrases, or use your own words or phrases that best express your wishes for yourself:

- *May I be safe and free from harm.*

- *May I be happy.*

- *May I be healthy and well.*

- *May I live with ease.*

As you repeat the phrases, hold an image of yourself in your mind and heart, wishing yourself well. If positive or pleasant feelings arise in your body or mind, take in these feelings and appreciate them, allowing them to grow as you repeat the phrases.

If feelings of resistance come up, meet them with kindness and friendliness. You can place your hand on your heart and acknowledge the resistance or difficult feeling. If it's difficult to wish yourself well, you might bring to mind an image of yourself as a baby or young child, who wants to be safe, loved, and happy, and continue to send wishes of loving-kindness to yourself. Hold whatever arises in a spirit of kindness and care.

After directing loving-kindness toward yourself, bring to mind a dear friend or loved one—someone who has cared deeply for you—and let his or her image come into your heart and mind. Slowly repeat the loving-kindness phrases for this person, as if you were speaking to him or her:

- *May you be safe and free from harm.*

- *May you be happy.*

- *May you be healthy and well.*

- *May you live with ease.*

As you repeat the phrases, take in and experience any feelings that arise. Use the words, the images in your mind, and the feelings that arise to deepen your intention of wishing well to this dear friend or loved one.

When you feel ready, expand your field of loving-kindness outward—first include other friends and acquaintances; then people you don't know; then those with whom you have some difficulty or conflict; then others near and far, including creatures of the air, land, and water; and finally all beings.

Loving-kindness meditation is an art rather than a set formula. You can use whatever words, feelings, images, and practices allow your heart to open to yourself and others. This might include beginning with a loved one and then sending wishes of loving-kindness to yourself. Or you can drop the words completely and simply rest with the intentions and feelings.

I recommend that you practice loving-kindness meditation for fifteen minutes daily or as often as you're able, gradually extending the length of your meditation to thirty minutes or longer. (A downloadable loving-kindness practice is available at the publisher's website: http://www.newharbinger

.com/32370.) You can also bring the practice into your daily life: you can send wishes of loving-kindness and well-being to your fellow passengers on a bus, train, or plane, or you can send wishes of loving-kindness and well-being to a work colleague who pushes your buttons.

In recent years, scientific studies have shown that loving-kindness meditation has significant benefits. Emma Seppälä, of Stanford University's Center for Compassion and Altruism Research and Education, highlighted eighteen science-based reasons to try loving-kindness meditation (Seppälä 2014). Here are some examples:

- People who practiced loving-kindness meditation increased their positive emotions, which, in turn, produced increases in their personal resources (for example, more purpose in life, social support, and decreased illness symptoms) (Fredrickson et al. 2008).

- A twenty-minute loving-kindness meditation led to a 33 percent decrease in pain and a 43 percent reduction in emotional tension among chronic migraine sufferers (Tonelli and Wachholtz 2014).

- A study of people with chronic low back pain showed significant reductions in pain, anger, and psychological distress among participants in an eight-week loving-kindness program (Carson et al. 2005).

- A twelve-week loving-kindness meditation program significantly reduced depression and post-traumatic stress disorder (PTSD) symptoms among veterans diagnosed with PTSD (Kearney et al. 2013).

- A pilot study of individuals with schizophrenia-spectrum disorders found that loving-kindness meditation was associated with decreased schizophrenic symptoms and increased positive emotions and psychological recovery (Johnson et al. 2011).

- Other studies have linked loving-kindness meditation to greater relaxation and less stress (Law 2011); increased empathy (Klimecki et al. 2013); decreased bias against minorities (Kang, Gray, and Dovido 2014); and reduced signs of aging in women (Hoge et al. 2013) and have shown that even a few minutes of loving-kindness meditation increased feelings of social connection and positivity toward strangers (Hutcherson, Seppälä, and Gross 2008).

Self-Compassion

One of the most important qualities you can cultivate to help change unhealthy habit patterns and develop more helpful ones is self-compassion, a quality of meeting your experience with kindness and without judgment while recognizing that your difficulties are part of the suffering shared by all humans. Interest in self-compassion has grown dramatically in recent years as research has demonstrated the benefits of compassion toward self and others. In 2009, Google Scholar reported 37,500 scholarly citations to publications containing the term "compassion," up from fewer than 5,000 in 1990 (Jazaieri et al. 2014, 23–24).

If you're pulled toward a habitual behavior—say, wanting something to satisfy an urge or moving toward distraction—the practice of self-compassion invites you to cultivate feelings of kindness toward yourself and to meet your experience nonjudgmentally, recognizing that you're not alone in experiencing these feelings and wishing to alleviate your own suffering.

Self-compassion can also help you respond constructively to "lapses," or when you revert to old habits. For example, if you're trying to give up smoking and you smoke a cigarette under stress, you might feel judgmental toward yourself, but you can choose to respond to the lapse with self-compassion and commit to refraining from acting on the urge the next time the temptation to smoke arises.

Kristin Neff, a professor at the University of Texas at Austin and a leading writer and researcher on self-compassion, defines self-compassion as entailing three key components:

1. *Self-kindness*—being gentle and understanding toward yourself rather than critical and judgmental

2. Recognizing your *common humanity*—feeling connected with others rather than feeling isolated and alienated

3. *Mindfulness*—holding your experience in balanced awareness rather than either identifying with it or avoiding it

Neff has developed a scale that measures individuals' ability to treat themselves with compassion, based on responses to questions related to these three key components.

Using Neff's scale—called the Self-Compassion Scale, or SCS—studies have found that higher levels of compassion were associated with lower levels of mental health problems. A review of twenty studies involving 4,007 participants found "empirical evidence for…the importance of self-compassion for developing well-being, reducing depression and anxiety, and increasing resilience to stress" (MacBeth and Gumley 2012, 550).

Other studies have found that self-compassion has the following benefits:

- It deactivates the body's stress response and activates the caregiving response (Gilbert and Procter 2006). This may lead to an increased feeling of being supported, as if by a loved one, contributing to emotional resilience.

- It's "associated with psychological strengths such as happiness, optimism, wisdom, curiosity and exploration, personal initiative and emotional intelligence" (Neff and Germer 2013, 29).

- It decreases cortisol—a stress-related hormone—and heart-rate variability, which is linked to less rumination, less perfectionism, and less fear of failure (Neff and Germer 2013).

- It promotes health-related behaviors such as sticking to one's diet, exercising, reducing smoking, and seeking needed medical treatment (Neff and Germer 2013).

The good news is that self-compassion, like mindfulness, can be developed and deepened through training and practice. Kristin Neff and Christopher Germer found that an eight-week mindful self-compassion program they developed raised participants' self-compassion levels by 43 percent (Germer and Neff 2013).

Practice 14: Self-Compassion Meditation

This meditation follows a similar format to the loving-kindness meditation, but with the emphasis on cultivating compassion toward yourself.

Begin by sitting in a relaxed and comfortable posture—or you can practice this meditation walking in a quiet place. Take some moments to relax and let go of any tension in your body and mind by taking some full breaths, relaxing any areas of tension, and inviting a smile to the corners of your eyes and mouth.

Bring a kind attention to any suffering you may be experiencing—sadness, loneliness, fear, hurt, or worry—and meet your feelings with kindness and care. Let go of any story or mental narrative about why you're feeling sad or lonely, and be open to the feelings you're experiencing.

Open yourself to the bodily feelings that are present with kindness and acceptance. You can place your hand on your heart and hold the painful feelings that are present with kindness. Set an intention to meet the painful feelings with care, compassion, and understanding.

Know that you're not alone—that even at this moment, others, too, are experiencing difficulties, pain, and loss. Whatever you're feeling is a shared human experience. Now repeat these phrases to yourself with kindness:

- *May I be safe.*

- *May I be happy.*

- *May I be kind to myself.*

- *May I accept myself as I am.*

As you repeat the phrases, be open to whatever bodily sensations arise, meeting anything you experience with kindness and acceptance. Whenever your mind wanders, gently bring your attention back to repeating the phrases or to the bodily feelings that are present.

If this practice evokes intense feelings or emotions, come back to awareness of your breathing, and when you feel ready, return to the phrases of self-compassion.

Finally, sit quietly for a few minutes, being open to whatever feelings or sensations are present. Take in any feelings of kindness toward yourself that arise, and if no feelings come up, or if you experience negative or difficult emotions, meet these with kindness and acceptance, appreciating the effort and intention you have brought to this practice.

Taking In the Good—Summing Up

Challenging emotions, such as sadness, anger, fear, and loneliness, can trigger habits that don't serve your well-being. Such emotions can spur you to eat or drink in unhealthy ways, smoke, check out from reality, or get lost in stressful thoughts as you seek ways to avoid the difficult emotions.

Studies show that "positive" emotions can neutralize the effects of "negative" emotions and can help you be open to a broader range of responses to a given situation, allowing you to overcome stressors and become more resilient. Cultivating emotions that broaden and expand your range of options, such as compassion and forgiveness, will also help you change your habits, because they'll help you not view a "lapse" as a failure and thus not give up.

For thousands of years, people have used the practices of loving-kindness and self-compassion to cultivate kindness and care toward themselves and others, as well as to counter the effects of painful emotions and mind states. Recent scientific studies support these age-old meditation practices, showing that they provide benefits for a wide variety of people and promote healthy behaviors such as exercising and quitting smoking.

CHAPTER 10

CHAPTER 10

Breaking Harmful Habits in Your Relationships and the Wider World

No one is born hating another person because of the color of his skin, or his background, or his religion. People must learn to hate, and if they can learn to hate, they can be taught to love, for love comes more naturally to the human heart than its opposite.

—Nelson Mandela, *Long Walk to Freedom: The Autobiography of Nelson Mandela*

In this chapter, we'll discuss harmful habits that can arise in your communications, particularly in situations of conflict, and collective habitual patterns of thought and behavior (that you may absorb) that can lead to suffering.

Bringing Mindfulness to Habits in Your Relationships

As ways in which your individual brain and nervous system have made certain patterns of thought and behavior automatic through repetition, your habits are highly personal. But habits also are deeply relational. We're quintessentially social beings, and our thoughts and actions develop in relationship with others—our caregivers, our family, our friends, our community, and the wider world. As such, our habits are often rooted in our childhood experiences. For example, in response to not feeling loved or emotionally nurtured, some children develop a habit of soothing themselves with food. Children who fear their parents will be angry if they tell the truth sometimes develop a habit of lying or evasion and then maintain this habit when confronted by any authority figure or whenever they feel under pressure. Children raised in a family where gossip about neighbors or outbursts of anger are the norm may find themselves as adults falling into these same habits of speech.

What's more, unhealthy habits are often strengthened and perpetuated in relationships. For example, if you have a habit of drinking excessively with particular friends, this habit may be triggered whenever you're with those friends. Not only that, but people who share a close relationship (for example, partners, spouses, and family members) often know what buttons to push in each other and can trigger predictable and habitual responses that perpetuate strife.

Using the skills and practices presented in the previous seven chapters, you can transform these patterns—for example, by learning to stay with difficult feelings, rather than acting them out, and by bringing awareness to and choosing not to identify with beliefs that perpetuate an unhealthy habit.

Mindful Communication in Situations of Conflict

A particularly important area where unhealthy habits can cause suffering in relationships is in your communications: how you use language to express your feelings and get your needs met.

Unhealthy habits of communication can deepen conflict rather than generate harmony. We can use words to generalize, criticize, judge, blame, make demands of, and attack one another rather than make specific observations, acknowledge our own emotions, and work together. You can transform your own unhealthy habits of communication by bringing awareness to these patterns and using language that contributes to harmony rather than to conflict and division.

An approach that I find powerful and effective for transforming habits of communication and cultivating harmony and understanding in relationships—particularly where there's conflict—is the practice of *nonviolent communication*, developed by psychologist Marshall Rosenberg (Rosenberg 2003).

Nonviolent communication provides a framework for cultivating wise communication and involves:

1. Using the language of *observation* rather than evaluation or judgment

   Rather than telling a friend who's late for your weekly lunch date "You're always late," you might point out that this is the third time she's arrived more than fifteen minutes after your agreed meeting time. When you speak in the language of observation, you can discuss what actually happened or is happening rather than focusing on the other person's character or making broad generalizations.

2. Expressing what you're *feeling*

    For example, "I felt embarrassed and annoyed when you made that remark about me to the group," rather than "You humiliated me in front of the group; I'll never trust you again." When you express what you're feeling, you speak about your direct experience rather than blaming or attacking the other person. This allows the other person to know how you're feeling without putting him or her on the defensive.

3. Recognizing what your *needs* are

    In any situation of conflict, you have needs that you're trying to meet. The other person also has needs that he or she is seeking to satisfy. Your need might be for connection, clarity, safety, self-respect, or something else you wish for. Nonviolent communication is a way of working toward meeting both parties' needs. When you investigate your own needs, you can get below the level of your habitual views and judgments to connect with what you're seeking in the situation. And when you acknowledge the other person's needs, the other person will feel heard and understood, and there's a greater possibility of both of you getting your needs met.

4. Making *requests*—asking for what you want, rather than making demands or being vague about what you're seeking

For example, "Would you be willing to call me and let me know if you're going to be home late?" When you request what you need, you give the other person the opportunity to say yes or no. And if the response is no, you can explore other ways of meeting your needs.

When you reflect on your own habits of communication, can you see patterns that lead to conflict and division with others? In a political discussion or debate, do you attack the other person instead of engaging with his or her ideas or policies? Do you find yourself using the language of "never" and "always" when describing the actions of your partner, spouse, or family member—for example, "She's always late" or "He never follows through"? Do you speak in the language of judgment rather than observation—for example, "He's so unreliable" or "You can't trust her"? Do you make demands or issue ultimatums (which can lead people to become defensive or resistant)?

Using a process of mindful and compassionate communication such as nonviolent communication can help you transform unhealthy habits of communication that can otherwise fuel conflict, misunderstanding, and division in your relationships.

Because your patterns of communication have developed over a lifetime, changing these habits takes dedication and patience. It's fundamentally a practice of mindfulness supported by compassion toward yourself and others. You can use the skills you have learned in the previous seven chapters for transforming habits, supported by the skills of nonviolent communication, which are honed to bring mindfulness to your communications.

Applying Mindfulness to Shared Habits

The habits that we have discussed and worked with in this book so far have mainly involved choices you have made, in attempts to meet your needs, that became habits when repeated in consistent contexts. If these habits run counter to your true interests and intentions, it serves you to change them, and we have explored, at length, mindfulness skills that can help you change unhealthy habits.

But what about habits that form not as a result of your choices or your efforts to meet a particular need but because you have absorbed them—in the water we all drink, as it were?

From time immemorial, cultures and societies have passed on their traditional wisdom, religious practices and rituals, laws, moral norms, and histories from one generation to the next. Like healthy personal habits, many of these views, norms, and practices aren't a problem, and most children who grow up absorbing these views and behaviors become relatively well-balanced, compassionate citizens. But what if the socially sanctioned laws, moral norms, and behaviors perpetuate harm? Can you change these collective patterns of thought and behavior through mindfulness? For example, if you had been born into the dominant group in a slave-owning society or born white in South Africa under apartheid (the system of racial separation), you would have grown up in a society where the laws, norms, assumptions, and everyday behaviors legitimated inequality and injustice. Unless you had been raised in a family or subculture that questioned the dominant norms, you would have absorbed ideas and beliefs that perpetuated these unjust arrangements. Even the victims of social injustice sometimes internalize their oppressors' beliefs about their "inferiority."

Bringing awareness to unconscious collective habits, such as those that lead to suffering, can be more challenging than bringing awareness to an unhealthy personal habit. If you have a strong craving for something, your body, emotions, and thoughts will usually tell you that something is off-kilter, even if you have ways of shutting down or overriding that recognition. Similarly, if you have a habit of escaping into fantasies to avoid an unpleasant feeling, or of being caught up in incessant worrying or planning, signals from your body and mind—and often from people who are close to you—will typically let you know that something is amiss. It's much easier for collective patterns of thought and behavior to operate "under the radar." The views and beliefs you share with family members, peers, or society as a whole can be so deeply internalized that there's no clear signal that something is wrong. Because such habits, and the behaviors that they underlie, are "the sea we swim in," the views and behaviors of people around you will tend to reinforce the harmful collective view.

I used the examples of slave-owning societies and the apartheid system to illustrate how even extremely unjust societies can pass on norms of thought and behavior that are portrayed as "natural" or religiously sanctioned. These are extreme cases—and with the ease of worldwide communication today and prevailing international norms of human rights and social justice, it's more difficult for these kinds of systems to maintain legitimacy and for people living in these societies to remain oblivious to the prevailing harm. But in many cases, the suffering may be less obvious but no less real.

Take the issue of racial justice and equity in the United States today. As members of the dominant racial group, many white people today have been raised to believe they live in a "color-blind" society where there's equal opportunity, the "playing field" is relatively level, and racial domination and injustices are a thing of the past. But increasingly these views have been called into question, particularly in the aftermath of recent killings by police of black men.

When you possess privileges that come from being a member of a dominant group—whether due to your race, ethnicity, social class, gender, sexual orientation, mental or physical ability, or other characteristic—the natural tendency is to be unaware of the benefits and take them for granted. You're brought up to see these privileges as normal, nothing special. You may be oblivious to the fact that others don't receive the same benefits or advantages you do, because the laws and social norms proclaim equality for all. (For members of subordinate groups, however, the disadvantages they face are all too clear.) Or you may internalize the belief that you "deserve" different or better treatment than others—based, for example, on religious or quasi-scientific views that seek to explain and justify your privileged position. You may believe your success is due to your merits or efforts, rather than unseen privilege—as with someone who was "born on third base and thought he hit a triple."

Peggy McIntosh, a researcher at the Wellesley College Center for Research on Women, pointed to the "invisible knapsack" of privileges that come with being born white in the United States. She noted, "I was taught to see racism only in individual acts of meanness, not in invisible systems conferring dominance on my group" (McIntosh 1988).

In a 1988 essay, McIntosh identified fifty privileges that she received by being white: "As far as I can tell, my African-American coworkers, friends, and acquaintances...cannot count on most of these conditions." These privileges included (in her words):

- "I can go shopping alone most of the time, pretty well assured that I will not be followed or harassed."

- "I can turn on the television or open to the front page of the paper and see people of my race widely represented."

- "I can be sure that my children will be given curricular materials that testify to the existence of their race."

- "I am never asked to speak for all the people of my racial group."

- "If a traffic cop pulls me over or if the IRS audits my tax return, I can be sure I haven't been singled out because of my race."

- "I can be late to a meeting without having the lateness reflect on my race."

- "I can arrange my activities so that I will never have to experience feelings of rejection owing to my race."

Unseen privileges help perpetuate harm and may be particularly challenging to identify and abandon. But any situation in which there's inequity and injustice harms members of both dominant and subordinate groups. If you want to cultivate inner peace, as well as greater harmony in the world, you need to bring these collective habits into the light of your awareness. The first step is humility—acknowledging that you don't know what you don't know. You can begin by bringing awareness and a spirit of inquiry to what you believe and asking yourself the questions that follow.

- *Is this belief true?*

- *Am I acting in ways that are based on assumptions that lead to harm to others or myself?*

- *Does this belief or action lead to well-being, or does it lead to harm?*

Be mindful of what may be going on outside the frame of your awareness. Curiosity and investigation are essential. Read, watch, and listen to opposing viewpoints, and ask yourself:

- *What am I not aware of?*

- *What am I missing?*

- *Where is there suffering? And what is its cause?*

It's also important to search out voices and opinions that may be less or rarely heard, especially those coming from marginalized or excluded groups. You can use the skills of mindfulness and practices of self-compassion and forgiveness to help you hold, with kindness, painful reactions that may arise when you open yourself to what was formerly hidden from your view. You can work with others who are also seeking healing and reconciliation, supporting one another in deepening the inquiry into how to awaken from the trance of harmful collective habits. As an example, in my meditation community we formed a white awareness group, dedicated to inquiring into privilege and racial justice and seeking to be part of a process of healing and reconciliation.

Mindfulness leads to wise and compassionate action. In an old Zen story, a student comes to visit his dying teacher. The student asks, "What is the teaching of your entire lifetime?" The teacher replies, "An appropriate response." Any time you become aware that your ways of seeing and acting are leading to harm, mindfulness will help you determine a wise and compassionate response. For example, if you notice you're stressed out and believing your stressful thoughts, with mindfulness you can bring awareness to your thoughts, choose to see them as thoughts rather than as "the truth," and can let them go.

The practices of mindfulness in this book will give you the skills to bring awareness to habits that cause harm, to stay with the feelings that are present (rather than resisting or running away), and to choose actions that promote your own and others' well-being and harmony. In the case of harmful collective habits, you need to engage in a broader level of investigation to bring the harm into awareness and transform it.

Breaking Harmful Habits in Your Relationships and the Wider World— Summing Up

Habits are personal and unique to each of us in that they're ways in which our patterns of thought and behavior become automatic through repetition. As you have seen, mindfulness can help you transform habits of all kinds through meeting your experience with a kind and nonjudging awareness.

Two additional areas call for particular attention and can also be changed with mindful awareness: habits that develop in relationships, particularly in communications in situations of conflict; and shared habitual patterns of thought and behavior that we're very often oblivious to.

An approach to habits of communication that can be particularly valuable in situations of conflict is *nonviolent communication*, an approach developed by the late Marshall Rosenberg. Nonviolent communication provides a framework for cultivating wise and compassionate speech and involves (1) using the language of observation rather than evaluation or judgment; (2) expressing honestly what you're feeling; (3) recognizing what your needs are and seeking ways to meet these and the other person's needs; and (4) making requests rather than demands.

Using a process of mindful and compassionate communication can help you transform unhealthy habits of communication that can otherwise fuel conflict and misunderstanding in your relationships.

You can also bring mindfulness to shared habits that you have absorbed from the broader society or groups that you're a part of. These habits can be particularly hard to change, because they're due less to personal choice than to the norms, values, and ideas of the groups that you're a part of. Harmful patterns of thought and behavior are often rooted in the benefits and privileges that come with being a member of a dominant group. Bringing mindfulness to what you're oblivious to calls for compassionate awareness, humility, curiosity, investigation, and working closely with others who are committed to healing the shared suffering that arises from social inequity and injustice.

CONCLUSION

Making Mindfulness Your Default Habit

Throughout this book, I have emphasized that you can change unhealthy habits and that mindfulness is a key to change—to living a life free of unnecessary stress and suffering.

Mindfulness will help you discern whether your habitual pattern of behavior or thought will serve your best interest or whether it will lead to harm. This opens up the possibility of choosing your response to your urges rather than acting mindlessly, out of habit.

Without awareness, you'll continue to be a prisoner of your old choices and your entrenched habits, repeating shop-worn patterns. Using the skills and practices presented in this book, you can train your mind so that mindfulness becomes your default mode, replacing conditioned habits as your way of being in the world.

Mindfulness is available to anyone, anywhere, at any time. All you need is to know that you can "come home"—to your direct experience, here and now—and build your capacity to be present by training your mind.

To bring mindfulness to any situation, you can ask yourself three questions:

1. *What am I aware of—what am I experiencing right now?*

2. *Can I say yes to this moment just as it is?*

3. *What's a wise and appropriate response?*

You can then choose to respond to the situation—or simply choose not to act—in a way that leads to genuine happiness rather than reacting automatically and habitually. All of your harmful habits can be transformed when met in this way with kindness and awareness.

That's not to say it's easy. It requires practice. Someone once said, "There's no such thing as a one-walk dog." That is, walking the dog isn't something you do once and never have to think about again. Dogs need to be walked daily if they're to stay healthy, and it's the same with your brain and practicing mindfulness.

Your habits have developed through repetition over time, and your brain has formed neural pathways that encourage further repetition. So, to retrain your mind, you need *healthy repetition*: letting old paths fall into disuse and forming new ones based on healthy choices that serve your true interests.

The fruit of mindfulness is that you can live as you truly wish to live. You can go beyond feelings of neediness or the illusion that things need to be a certain way for you to be happy. You can live with a quality of ease that you never thought possible amid life's challenges.

Here are six tips to help you make mindfulness your default habit in daily life:

1. Establish a daily meditation practice.

   Begin by reflecting and writing down why establishing a daily meditation practice is important to you. You might consider telling a family member or a friend that you're making a commitment to meditate every day, so that you're accountable to another person for being true to your word. Commit to meditate each day for a week, and then commit for another week. Find a consistent time and place to meditate—this supports making the practice into a healthy habit. You can begin with ten or fifteen minutes and increase the amount of time as you feel ready. Set a timer or alarm so that you don't have to be concerned with how many more minutes you have left to go. Use the guided meditations in this book (or others) to help support your practice.

2. Use a notebook to keep a record of your meditations—how long you sat for, as well as what was most notable in your experience (for example, restlessness or tiredness or feeling calm and peaceful) or what you noticed during the meditation period.

   If difficulties came up, you might reflect on how you'll meet similar challenges if they arise in the future. Use the meditations in this book to work with specific difficulties as appropriate.

3. Take time during the day to pause—bringing awareness to your breath, your bodily feelings, and your overall state of body and mind.

   You might pause for three full breath cycles, bringing attention to whatever is present and saying yes to it. Or take five minutes to come home to yourself, simply recognizing and allowing whatever is present. You can set a timer (or download a "mindfulness bell") on your smartphone or computer to remind you to pause at regular or random intervals.

4. Envision moments you know will come up in daily life, and be prepared to use those times to be fully present.

    For example, whenever you're driving and you're stopped at a red light, take a "mindful pause." Whenever you're waiting in line at a store, be grateful for the opportunity to pause for a moment and bring mindfulness to your breath and body. If you're on a bus or other form of public transport, you can use the "I am aware of..." practice in chapter 4 to note what's coming up—sights, sounds, sensations, thoughts—or practice loving-kindness to all who are sharing the journey with you.

5. For a week, choose one activity to do mindfully and consciously each day.

    You might choose walking to your workplace or home, cooking or eating a meal, driving to work, washing up, or taking a shower. Whatever you choose, give this activity your undivided attention. See how you feel when you engage in this activity with full awareness.

6. Find a community of people to meditate with regularly—at least weekly, if possible.

    Attend a regular meditation class or sitting group. Cultivate or deepen spiritual friendships with like-minded people who are committed to living with awareness. If there are no such groups near you, try to find one or two other people to meditate with regularly. You can also find meditation communities online.

Finally, one of the deepest truths of mindfulness—and life—is that *you can begin again in any moment*. You can open to this breath, this feeling, this moment, with a *beginner's mind*, letting any residue or baggage from the past or thoughts of the future fall away.

You can come back to the present—to these practices—at any time, anywhere. May these skills and practices that have served so many through the centuries help you find inner peace and freedom.

Acknowledgments

I 'm very grateful for the support of many people in writing this book. I want to thank and acknowledge all who helped improve the writing and organization of the book, including Jeremy Mohler, Joan Mooney, Susan Collins, Rimas Blekaitis, Brian Levy, Sophia Galvan, Grace Ogden, Rebecca Hines, and Barbara Graham; everyone at New Harbinger Publications, especially Wendy Millstine, Jess Beebe, Karen Hathaway, Vicraj Gill, and freelancer Will DeRooy; the friends, students, and fellow teachers of the Insight Meditation Community of Washington (IMCW), including founding teacher Tara Brach, who has been a mentor, dear friend, and source of support and wisdom; all the teachers and practitioners of meditation and mindfulness, going back to the time of the Buddha and beyond, who have committed to living an awakened life and helping heal the suffering of the world; the teachers who have played a profound role in making ancient wisdom teachings accessible to Western students and practitioners, particularly Jack Kornfield, Sharon Salzberg, and Joseph Goldstein; the teachers whose wisdom and clarity have supported my practice and teaching, including Ajahn Chah, Ven. Anālayo, Bhante Gunaratana, Suzuki Roshi, Pema Chödrön, Bhikkhu Bodhi, Thich Nhat Hanh, Tsoknyi Rinpoche, Larry Rosenberg, Christopher Titmuss, Jack Kornfield, Sharon Salzberg, Joseph Goldstein, Christina Feldman, Jon Kabat-Zinn, Tara Brach, Rick Hanson, Phillip Moffitt, Gil Fronsdal, Eckhart Tolle, and Adyashanti; and all who have provided love, friendship, and emotional support, including my daughter Emma, her husband John, my grand-children John, Hugh, and Eve, my son Joseph, my siblings and their partners and families, my mother, my late father, John Byrne, DFC, and my life partner, Rebecca Hines, who has been a rock of support and love throughout this journey.

References

Adams, C., W. Heppner, S. Houchins, D. Stewart, J. Vidrine, and D. Wetter. 2014. "Mindfulness Meditation and Addictive Behaviors." In *Psychology of Meditation*, edited by N. Singh. Hauppauge, NY: Nova Science Publishers.

Adyashanti. 2008. *The End of Your World: Uncensored Straight Talk on the Nature of Enlightenment*. Boulder, CO: Sounds True.

Anālayo (Ven.) 2003. *Satipatthāna: The Direct Path to Realization*. Birmingham, England: Windhorse Publications.

Avena, N., P. Rada, and B. Hoebel. 2008. "Evidence for Sugar Addiction: Behavioral and Neurochemical Effects of Intermittent, Excessive Sugar Intake." *Neuroscience and Biobehavioral Reviews* 32 (1): 20–39.

Batchelor, M. 2007. *Let Go: A Buddhist Guide to Breaking Free of Habits*. Boston: Wisdom Publications.

Begley, S. 2012, April 30. "As America's Waistline Expands, Costs Soar." Reuters.

Bodhi, B., trans. 1995. *The Middle Length Discourses of the Buddha: A New Translation of the Majjhima Nikāya*. Original translation by Bhikkhu Ñānamoli. Boston: Wisdom Publications.

Bowen, S., N. Chawla, and G. A. Marlatt. 2011. *Mindfulness-Based Relapse Prevention for Addictive Behaviors*. New York: Guilford Press.

Bowen, S., and G. A. Marlatt. 2009. "Surfing the Urge: Brief Mindfulness-Based Intervention for College Student Smokers." *Psychology of Addictive Behaviors* 23 (4): 666–71.

Brach, T. 2003. *Radical Acceptance: Embracing Your Life with the Heart of a Buddha.* New York: Bantam Books.

———. 2013. *True Refuge: Finding Peace and Freedom in Your Own Awakened Heart.* New York: Bantam Books.

Brewer, J., S. Mallik, T. Babuscio, C. Nich, H. Johnson, C. Deleone, et al. 2011. "Mindfulness Training for Smoking Cessation: Results from a Randomized Controlled Trial." *Drug and Alcohol Dependence* 119 (1): 72–80.

Carson, J., F. Keefe, T. Lynch, K. Carson, V. Goli, A. Fras, and S. Thorp. 2005. "Loving-Kindness Meditation for Chronic Low Back Pain: Results from a Pilot Trial." *Journal of Holistic Nursing* 23 (3): 287–304.

Chang, L. 2006. *Wisdom for the Soul: Five Millennia of Prescriptions for Spiritual Healing.* Washington, DC: Gnosophia Publishers.

Covey, S. 1998. *The 7 Habits of Highly Effective Teens: The Ultimate Teenage Success Guide.* New York: Simon & Schuster.

Duhigg, C. 2012. *The Power of Habit: Why We Do What We Do in Life and Business.* New York: Random House.

Ekman, P. 1994. "Moods, Emotions, and Traits." In *The Nature of Emotion: Fundamental Questions,* edited by P. Ekman and R. Davidson. New York: Oxford University Press.

Farb, N., Z. Segal, H. Mayberg, J. Bean, D. McKeon, Z. Fatima, and A. Anderson. 2007. "Attending to the Present: Mindfulness Meditation Reveals Distinct Neural Modes of Self-Reference." *Social Cognitive and Affective Neuroscience* 2 (4): 313–22.

Feldman, C. 2005. *Compassion: Listening to the Cries of the World.* Berkeley, CA: Rodmell Press.

Frankl, V. E. 2006. *Man's Search for Meaning.* Part One translated by I. Lasch. Boston: Beacon Press.

Fredrickson, B. 2000. "Cultivating Positive Emotions to Optimize Health and Well-Being." *Prevention and Treatment* 3 (1): n.p.

Fredrickson, B., M. Cohn, K. Coffey, J. Pek, and S. Finkel. 2008. "Open Hearts Build Lives: Positive Emotions, Induced Through Loving-Kindness Meditation, Build Consequential Personal Resources." *Journal of Personality and Social Psychology* 95 (5): 1045–62.

Fredrickson, B., and R. Levenson. 1998. "Positive Emotions Speed Recovery from the Cardiovascular Sequelae of Negative Emotions." *Cognition and Emotion* 12 (2): 191–220.

Gardner, B. 2012. "Habit as Automaticity, Not Frequency." *European Health Psychologist* 14 (2): 32–36.

Gardner, B., P. Lally, and J. Wardle. 2012. "Making Health Habitual: The Psychology of 'Habit-Formation' and General Practice." *British Journal of General Practice* 62 (605): 664–66.

Germer, C., and K. Neff. 2013. "Self-Compassion in Clinical Practice." *Journal of Clinical Psychology* 69 (8): 856–67.

Gilbert, P., and S. Procter. 2006. "Compassionate Mind Training for People with High Shame and Self-Criticism: Overview and Pilot Study of a Group Therapy Approach." *Clinical Psychology and Psychotherapy* 13 (6): 353–79.

Goldstein, J. 1993. *Insight Meditation: The Practice of Freedom.* Boston: Shambhala Publications.

Gollwitzer, P., and B. Schaal. 1998. "Metacognition in Action: The Importance of Implementation Intentions." *Personality and Social Psychology Review* 2 (2): 124–36.

Halsey, A., III. 2013, December 16. "Survey: Drivers Ignore Warnings About Risk of Texting and Cellphone Use While on the Road." *Washington Post.* http://www.washingtonpost.com/local/trafficandcommuting/survey-drivers-ignore-warnings-about-risk-of-texting-and-cellphone-use-while-on-the-road/2013/12/16/0978f75a-6677–11e3–8b5b-a77187b716a3_story.html.

Hanson, R. 2009. *Buddha's Brain: The Practical Neuroscience of Happiness, Love, and Wisdom*. With R. Mendius. Oakland, CA: New Harbinger Publications.

Hebb, D. O. 1949. *The Organization of Behavior: A Neuropsychological Theory*. New York: Wiley and Sons. Hebb's full statement, known as Hebb's Law, is: "When an axon of cell A is near enough to excite cell B and repeatedly or persistently takes part in firing it, some growth process or metabolic change takes place in one or both cells such that A's efficiency, as one of the cells firing B, is increased."

Hoge, E., M. Chen, E. Orr, C. Metcalf, L. Fischer, M. Pollack, I. De Vivo, and N. Simon. 2013. "Loving-Kindness Meditation Practice Associated with Longer Telomeres in Women." *Brain, Behavior, and Immunity* 32: 159–63.

Hölzel, B., J. Carmody, M. Vangel, C. Congleton, S. Yerramsetti, T. Gard, and S. Lazar. 2011. "Mindfulness Practice Leads to Increases in Regional Brain Gray Matter Density." *Psychiatry Research: Neuroimaging* 191 (1): 36–43.

Hunt, D. N. d. "Peace Is This Moment Without Judgment." http://www.dorothyhunt.org/poetry_page.htm.

Hutcherson, C., E. Seppälä, and J. Gross. 2008. "Loving-Kindness Meditation Increases Social Connectedness." *Emotion* 8 (5): 720–24.

Hutson, M. 2015, January 6. "Beyond Happiness: The Upside of Feeling Down." *Psychology Today*. https://www.psychologytoday.com/articles/201501/beyond-happiness-the-upside-feeling-down.

Jalāl al-Din Rumi, M. 2004. "The Guest House." *The Essential Rumi*. New expanded ed. Translations by C. Barks, with J. Moyne, A. J. Arberry, and R. Nicholson. New York: HarperCollins.

James, W. 1890. *The Principles of Psychology* (2 vols.). New York: Henry Holt (Reprinted Bristol: Thoemmes Press, 1999).

———. 1892. *Psychology*. New York: Henry Holt and Company.

Jazaieri, H., K. McGonigal, T. Jinpa, J. Doty, J. Gross, and P. Goldin. 2014. "A Randomized Controlled Trial of Compassion Cultivation Training: Effects on Mindfulness, Affect, and Emotion Regulation." *Motivation and Emotion* 38: 23–35.

Johnson, D., D. Penn, B. Fredrickson, A. Kring, P. Meyer, L. Catalino, and M. Brantley. 2011. "A Pilot Study of Loving-Kindness Meditation for the Negative Symptoms of Schizophrenia." *Schizophrenia Research* 129 (2): 137–40.

Kabat-Zinn, J. 1990. *Full Catastrophe Living: Using the Wisdom of Your Body and Mind to Face Stress, Pain, and Illness.* New York: Delta.

———. 2003. "Mindfulness-Based Interventions in Context: Past, Present and Future." *Clinical Psychology: Science and Practice* 10 (2): 144–56.

Kahneman, D. 2003. "A Perspective on Judgment and Choice: Mapping Bounded Rationality." *American Psychologist* 58 (9): 697–720.

———. 2011. *Thinking, Fast and Slow.* New York: Farrar, Straus and Giroux.

Kang, Y., J. Gray, and J. Dovido. 2014. "The Nondiscriminating Heart: Lovingkindness Meditation Training Decreases Implicit Intergroup Bias." *Journal of Experimental Psychology: General* 143 (3): 1306–13.

Katie, B. 2002. *Loving What Is: Four Questions That Can Change Your Life.* New York: Random House.

Kearney, D., C. Malte, C. McManus, M. Martinez, B. Felleman, and T. Simpson. 2013. "Loving-Kindness Meditation for Posttraumatic Stress Disorder: A Pilot Study." *Journal of Traumatic Stress* 26 (2): 426–34.

Klimecki, O., S. Leiberg, C. Lamm, and T. Singer. 2013. "Functional Neural Plasticity and Associated Changes in Positive Affect After Compassion Training." *Cerebral Cortex* 23 (7): 1552–61.

Kornfield, J. 1996. "Bahiya." Adapted from the Udana, translated by F. L. Woodward. In *Teachings of the Buddha*, edited by J. Kornfield, with G. Fronsdal. Rev. and expanded ed. Boston and London: Shambhala.

———. 2008. *The Wise Heart: A Guide to the Universal Teachings of Buddhist Psychology*. New York: Bantam Books.

Krishnamurti, J. N.d. *The Book of Life.* http://www.dasglueck.de/download/krishnamurti/The_Book_of_Life.pdf (Meditation for November 8).

Law, W. 2011. "An Analogue Study of Loving-Kindness Meditation as a Buffer Against Social Stress." Dissertation, University of Arizona.

Levine, P. 1997. *Waking the Tiger: Healing Trauma*. Berkeley, CA: North Atlantic Books.

MacBeth, A., and A. Gumley. 2012. "Exploring Compassion: A Meta-analysis of the Association Between Self-Compassion and Psychopathology." *Clinical Psychology Review* 32 (6): 545–52.

Mandela, N. 2013. *Long Walk to Freedom: The Autobiography of Nelson Mandela*. New York: Little, Brown and Company.

Marcus Aurelius. 2006. *Meditations*. Translated by M. Hammond. London: Penguin Classics.

Mason, M., M. Norton, J. Van Horn, D. Wegner, S. Grafton, and C. Macrae. 2007. "Wandering Minds: The Default Network and Stimulus-Independent Thought." *Science* 315 (5810): 393–95.

McGonigal, K. 2012. *The Neuroscience of Change*. Audio CD. Boulder, CO: Sounds True.

McIntosh, P. 1988. "White Privilege: Unpacking the Invisible Knapsack," excerpted from *White Privilege and Male Privilege: A Personal Account of Coming to See Correspondences through Work in Women's Studies*. Wellesley College Center for Research on Women. *Working Paper 189.*

Mischel, W. 2014. *The Marshmallow Test: Mastering Self-Control*. New York: Little, Brown and Company.

Moffitt, P. 2008. *Dancing with Life: Buddhist Insights for Finding Meaning and Joy in the Face of Suffering.* New York: Rodale.

Moore, A., and P. Malinowski. 2009. "Meditation, Mindfulness and Cognitive Flexibility." *Consciousness and Cognition* 18 (1): 176–86.

Morris, T., M. Spittle, and A. Watt. 2005. *Imagery in Sport.* Champaign, IL: Human Kinetics.

Moss, M. 2014. *Salt, Sugar, Fat: How the Food Giants Hooked Us.* New York: Random House.

National Institutes of Health (NIH), National Institute on Drug Abuse. 2012, November. *DrugFacts: Understanding Drug Abuse and Addiction.* http://www.drugabuse.gov/publica tions/drugfacts/understanding-drug-abuse-addiction.

Neff, K., and C. Germer. 2013. "A Pilot Study and Randomized Controlled Trial of the Mindful Self-Compassion Program." *Journal of Clinical Psychology* 69 (1): 28–44.

Neyfakh, L. 2013, November 3. "Texting and Driving: A Deadly Habit." *The Week.* http://theweek.com/articles/457554 /texting-driving-deadly-habit.

Nhat Hanh, Thich. 1975. *The Miracle of Mindfulness: An Introduction to the Practice of Meditation.* Boston: Beacon Press.

Nilsen, P., K. Roback, A. Broström, and P. Ellström. 2012. "Creatures of Habit: Accounting for the Role of Habit in Implementation Research on Clinical Behavior Change." *Implementation Science* 7 (53): 1–6.

Ouellette, J., and W. Wood. 1998. "Habit and Intention in Everyday Life: The Multiple Processes by Which Past Behavior Predicts Future Behavior." *Psychological Bulletin* 124 (1): 54–74.

Postlethwaite, M. "Clearing." Unpublished poem.

Prochaska, J., C. DiClemente, and J. Norcross. 1992. "In Search of How People Change: Applications to Addictive Behaviors." *American Psychologist* 47 (9): 1102–14.

Quinn, J., A. Pascoe, W. Wood, and D. Neal. 2010. "Can't Control Yourself? Monitor Those Bad Habits." *Personality and Social Psychology Bulletin* 36 (4): 499–511.

Rosenberg, M. 2003. *Nonviolent Communication: A Language of Life.* 2nd ed. Encinitas, CA: PuddleDancer Press.

Salzberg, S. 1995. *Lovingkindness: The Revolutionary Art of Happiness.* Boston: Shambhala Publications.

Seppälä, E. 2014, September 17. "18 Science-Based Reasons to Try Loving-Kindness Meditation." *Huffington Post.* http://www.huffingtonpost.com/emma-seppala-phd/18-science based-reasons-t_b_5823952.html.

Shapiro, S., L. Carlson, J. Astin, and B. Freedman. 2006. "Mechanisms of Mindfulness." *Journal of Clinical Psychology* 62 (3): 373–86.

Shihab Nye, N. 1995. "Kindness." *Words Under the Words: Selected Poems.* Portland, OR: Far Corner Books.

Suzuki, S. 1998. *Zen Mind, Beginner's Mind.* New York: Weatherhill.

Tolle, E. 2003. *Realizing the Power of Now: An In-Depth Retreat with Eckhart Tolle.* Audio CD. Boulder, CO: Sounds True.

Tonelli, M., and A. Wachholtz. 2014. "Meditation-Based Treatment Yielding Immediate Relief for Meditation-Naïve Migraineurs." *Pain Management Nursing* 15 (1): 36–40.

Trungpa, C. 1999. *The Essential Chögyam Trungpa.* Boston: Shambhala Publications.

Wood, W., J. Quinn, and D. Kashy. 2002. "Habits in Everyday Life: Thought, Emotion, and Action." *Journal of Personality and Social Psychology* 83: 1281–97.

Yongey Mingyur. 2007. *The Joy of Living: Unlocking the Secret and Science of Happiness.* With E. Swanson. New York: Harmony Books.

Hugh G. Byrne, PhD, is a guiding teacher with the Insight Meditation Community of Washington (IMCW), and cofounder of the Mindfulness Training Institute of Washington. He has worked extensively in the fields of human rights and social justice, and is committed to advocating the benefits of mindfulness and other contemplative practices to help relieve the suffering of the world. He teaches classes, retreats, and workshops in the United States and internationally. Byrne resides in Silver Spring, MD.

Foreword writer **Tara Brach, PhD**, has been practicing meditation since 1975 and leads Buddhist meditation retreats at centers in North America and Europe. She is a clinical psychologist and author of *Radical Acceptance* and *True Refuge*.

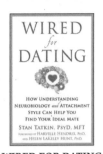

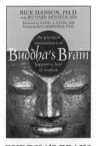
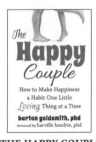

Register your **new harbinger** titles for additional benefits!

When you register your **new harbinger** title—purchased in any format, from any source—you get access to benefits like the following:

- Downloadable accessories like printable worksheets and extra content

- Instructional videos and audio files

- Information about updates, corrections, and new editions

Not every title has accessories, but we're adding new material all the time.

Access free accessories in 3 easy steps:

1. Sign in at NewHarbinger.com (or **register** to create an account).

2. Click on **register a book**. Search for your title and click the **register** button when it appears.

3. Click on the **book cover or title** to go to its details page. Click on **accessories** to view and access files.

That's all there is to it!

If you need help, visit:

NewHarbinger.com/accessories

new harbinger
CELEBRATING
40 YEARS